Happy Easter

Color me

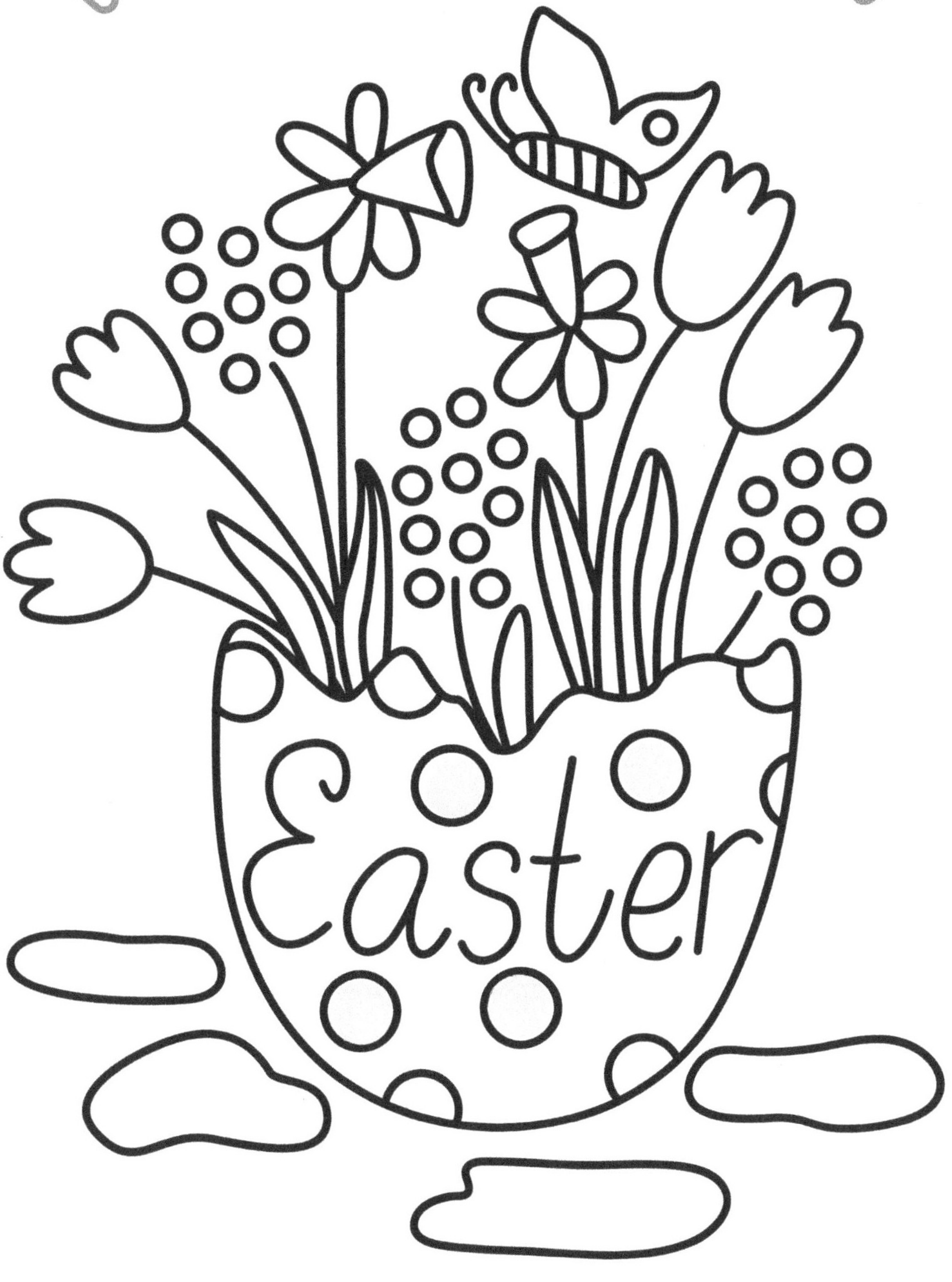

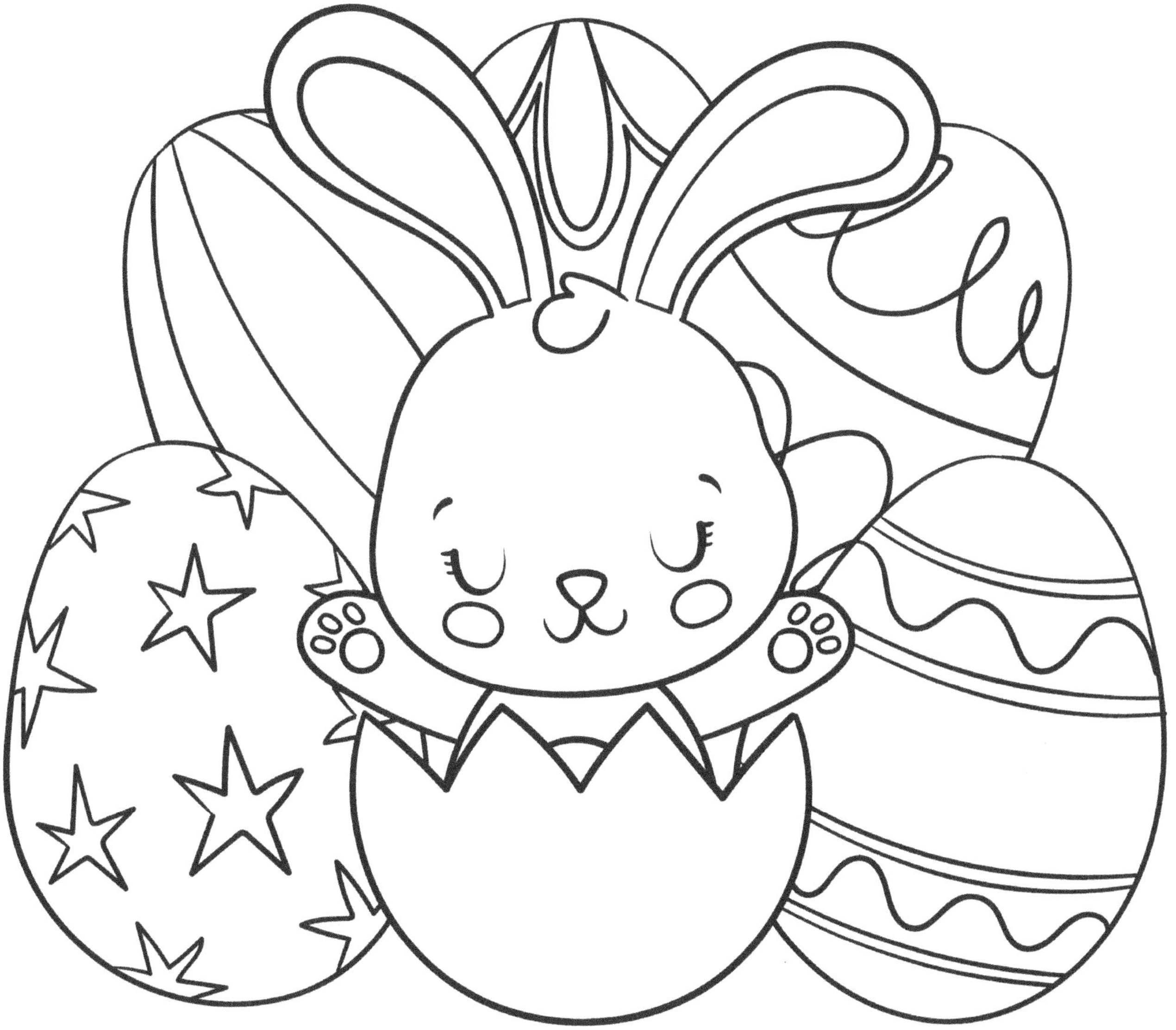

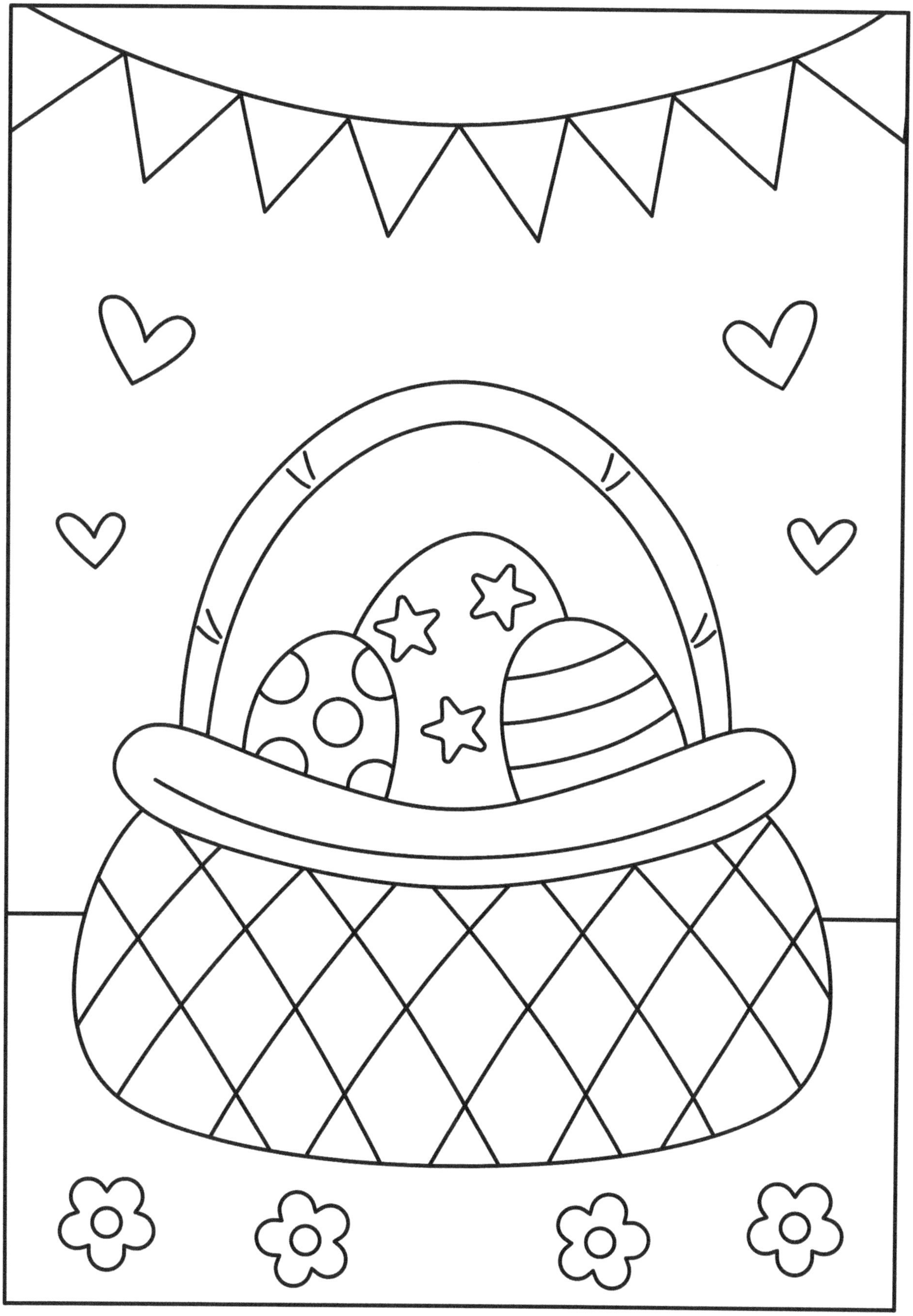

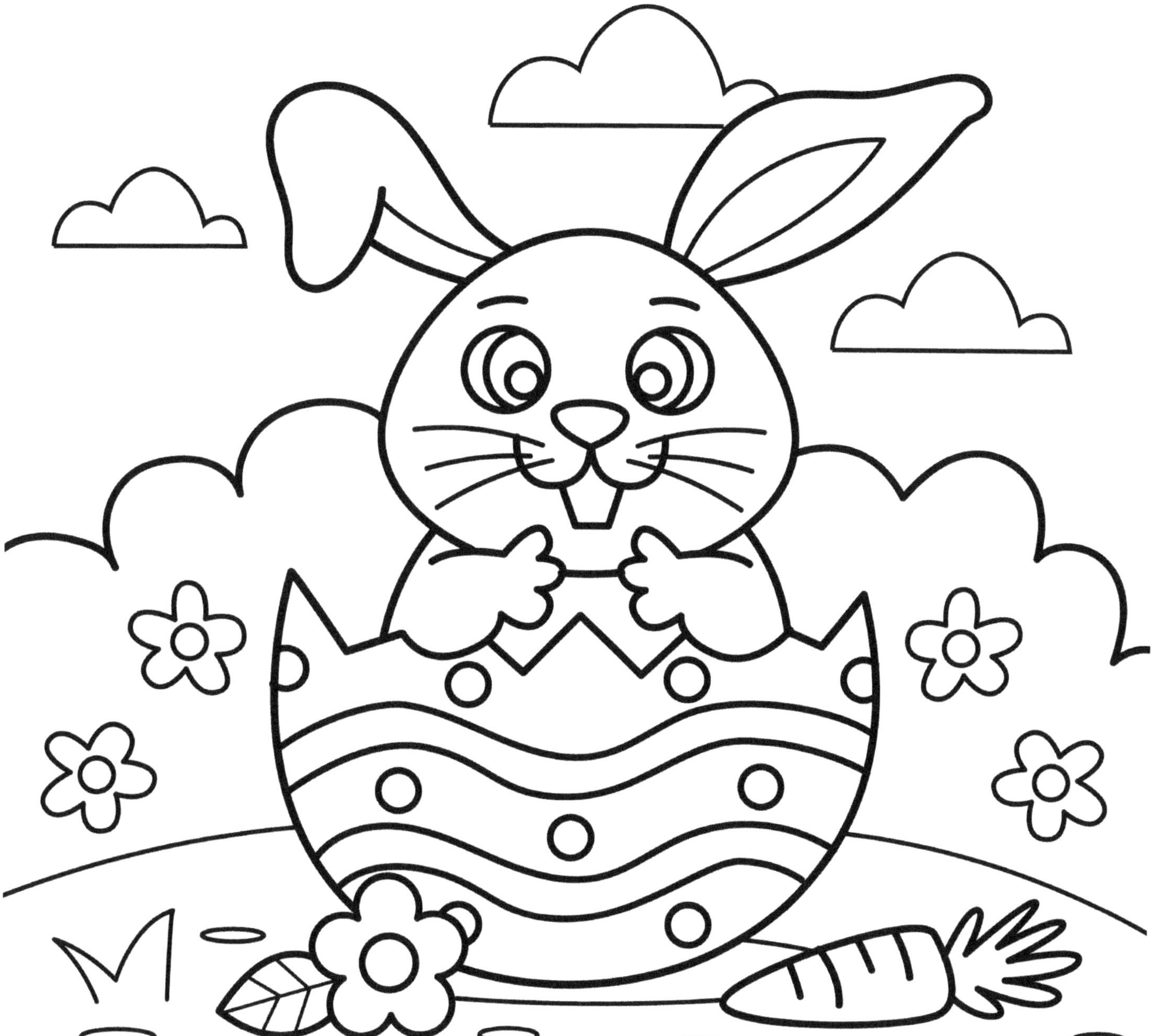

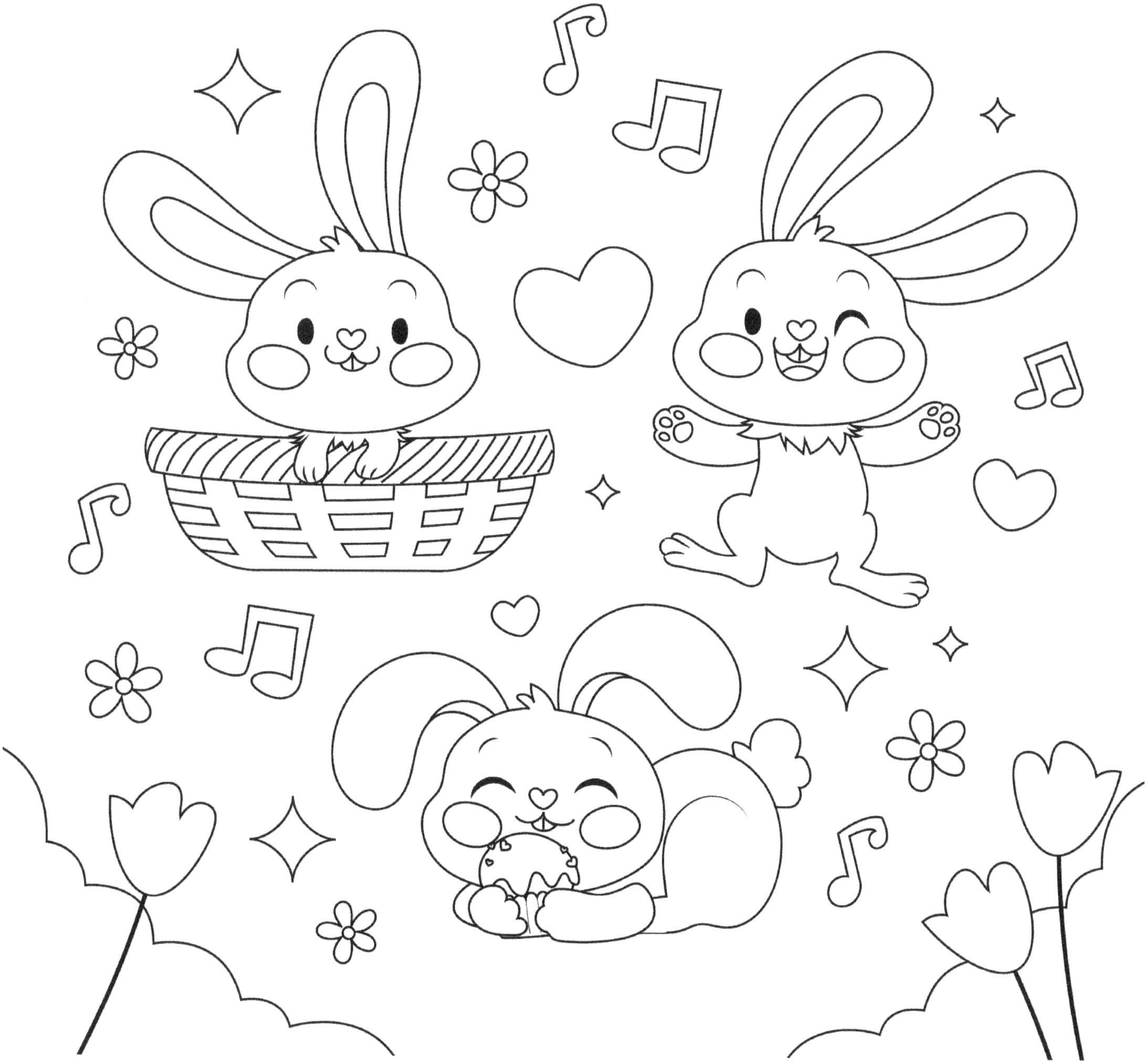

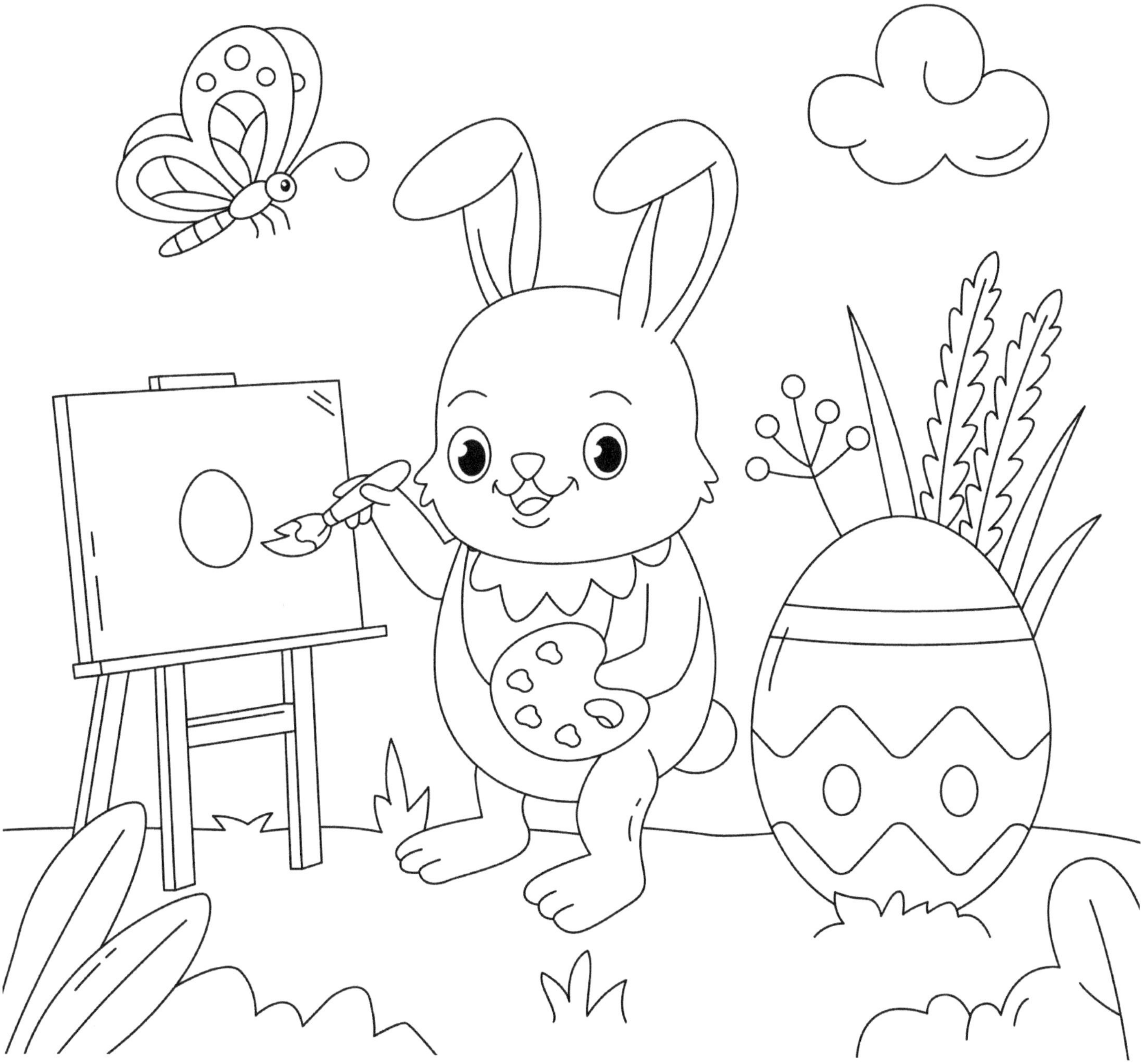

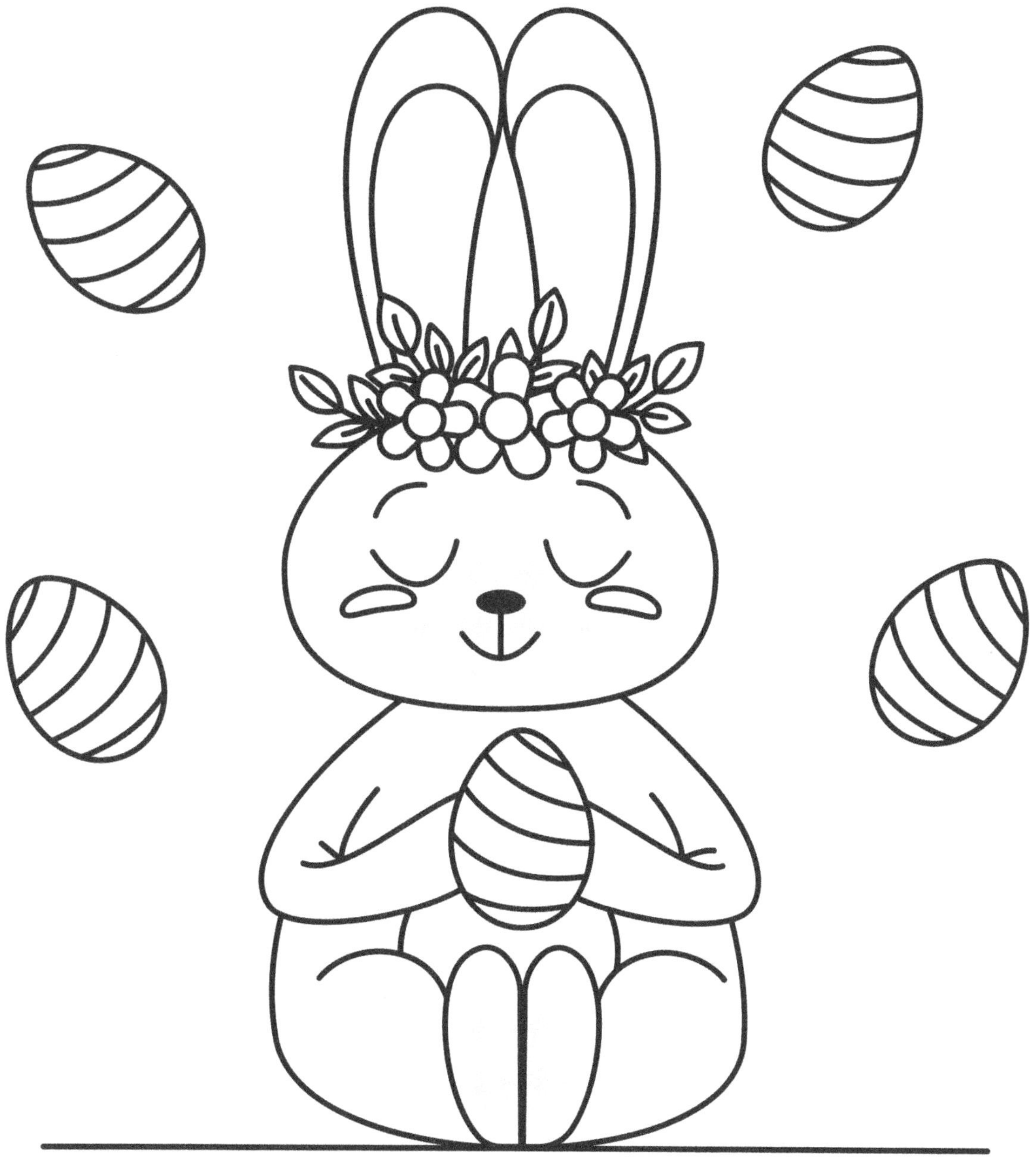

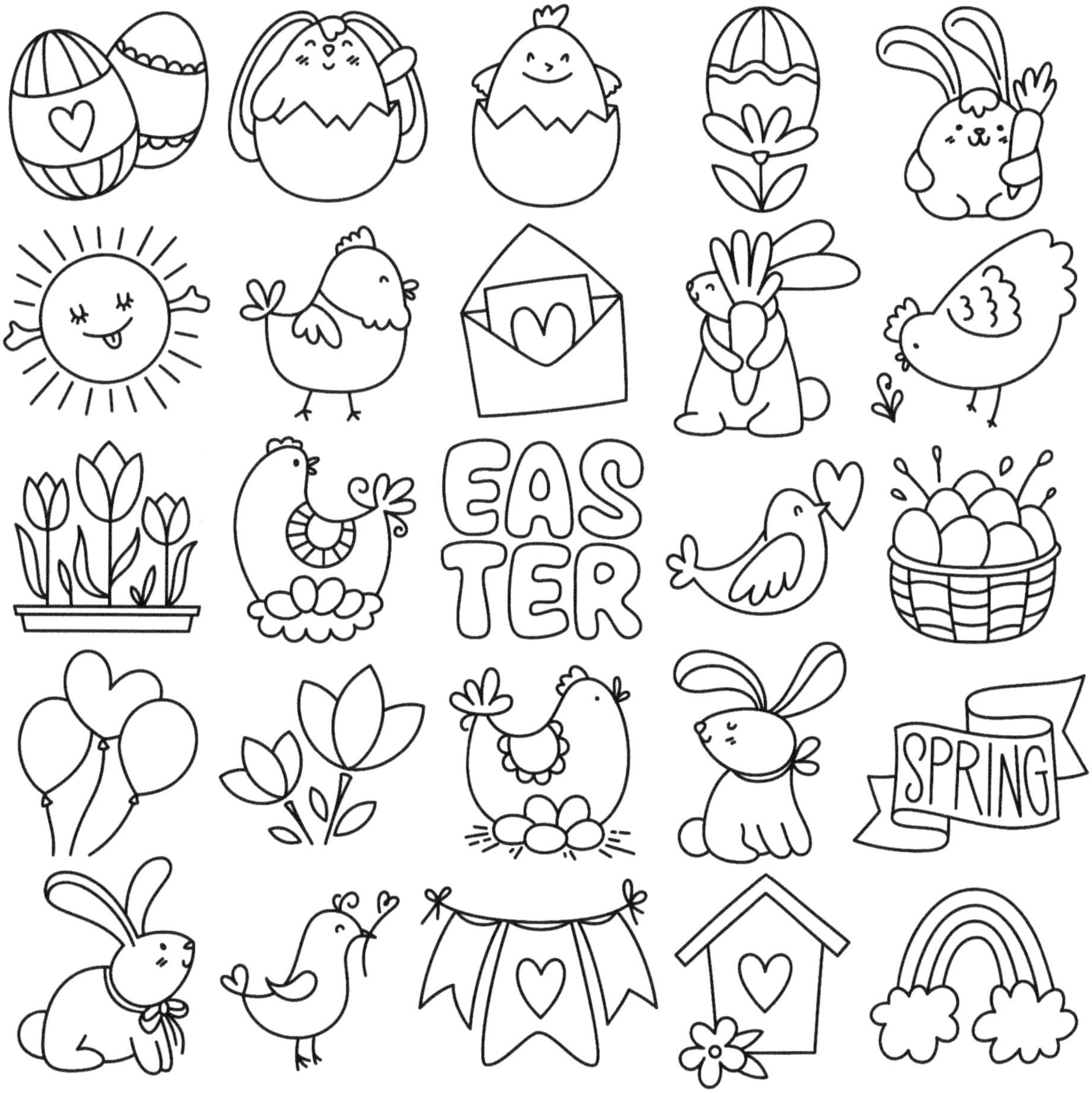
EAS
TER
SPRING

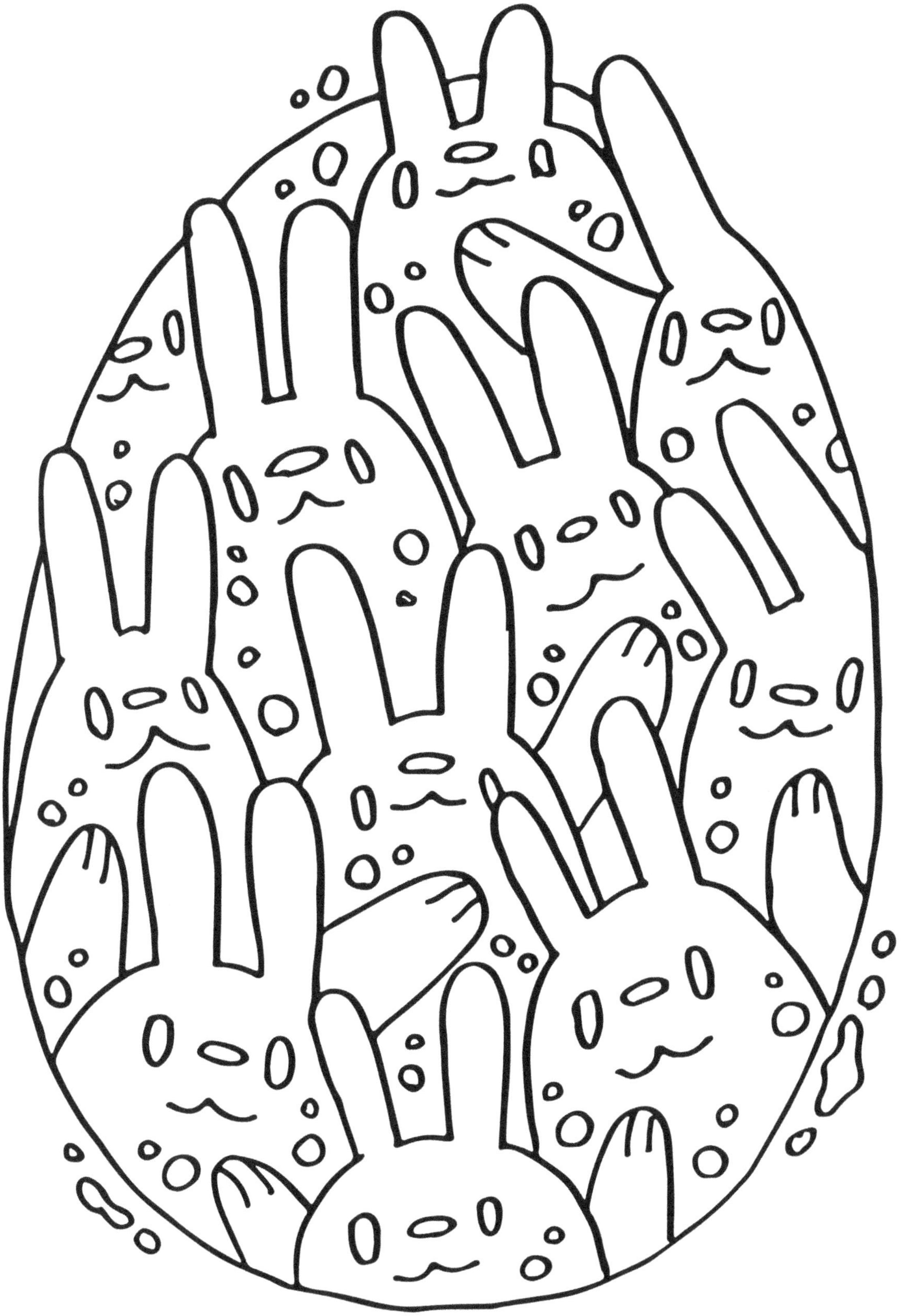

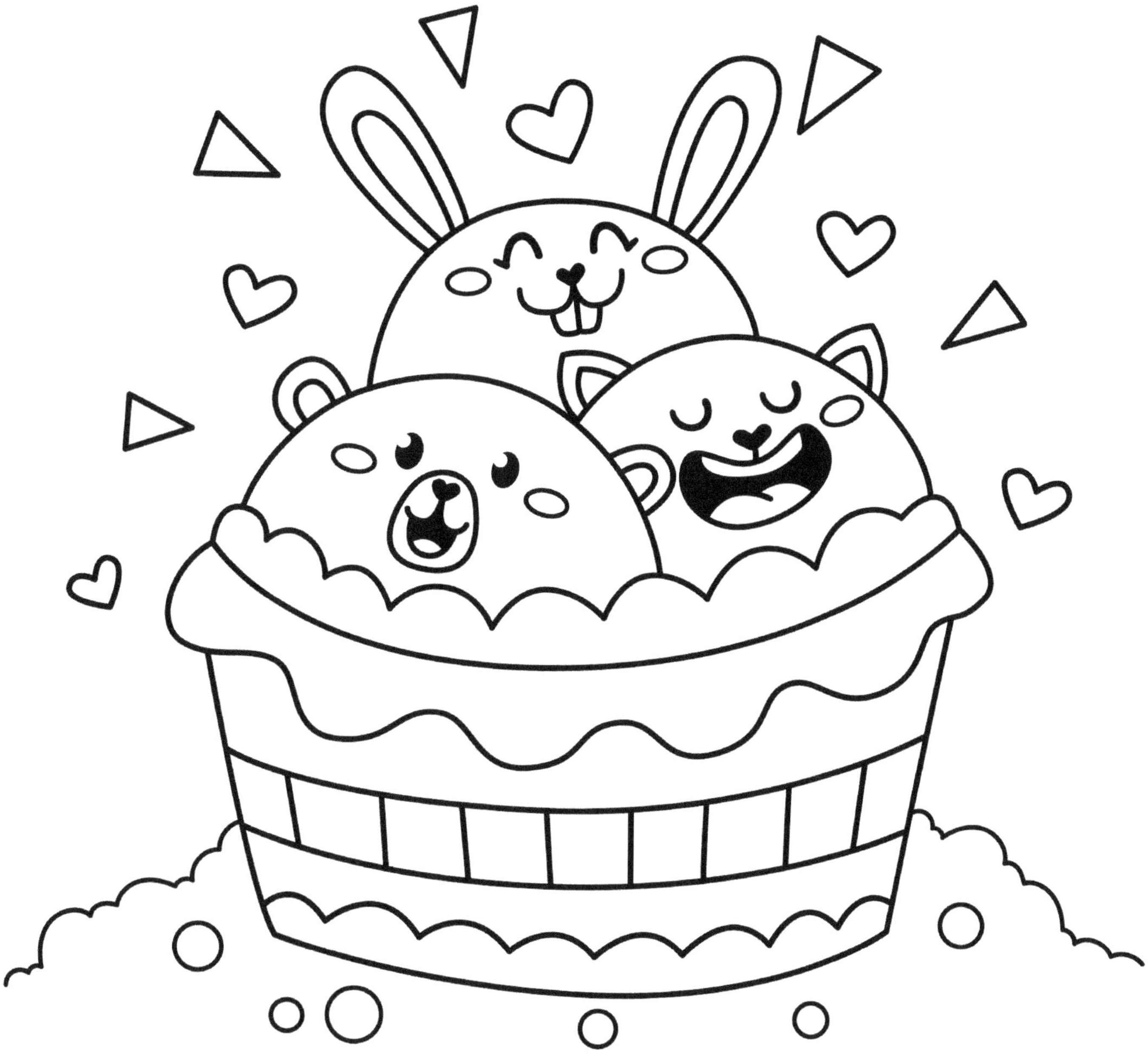

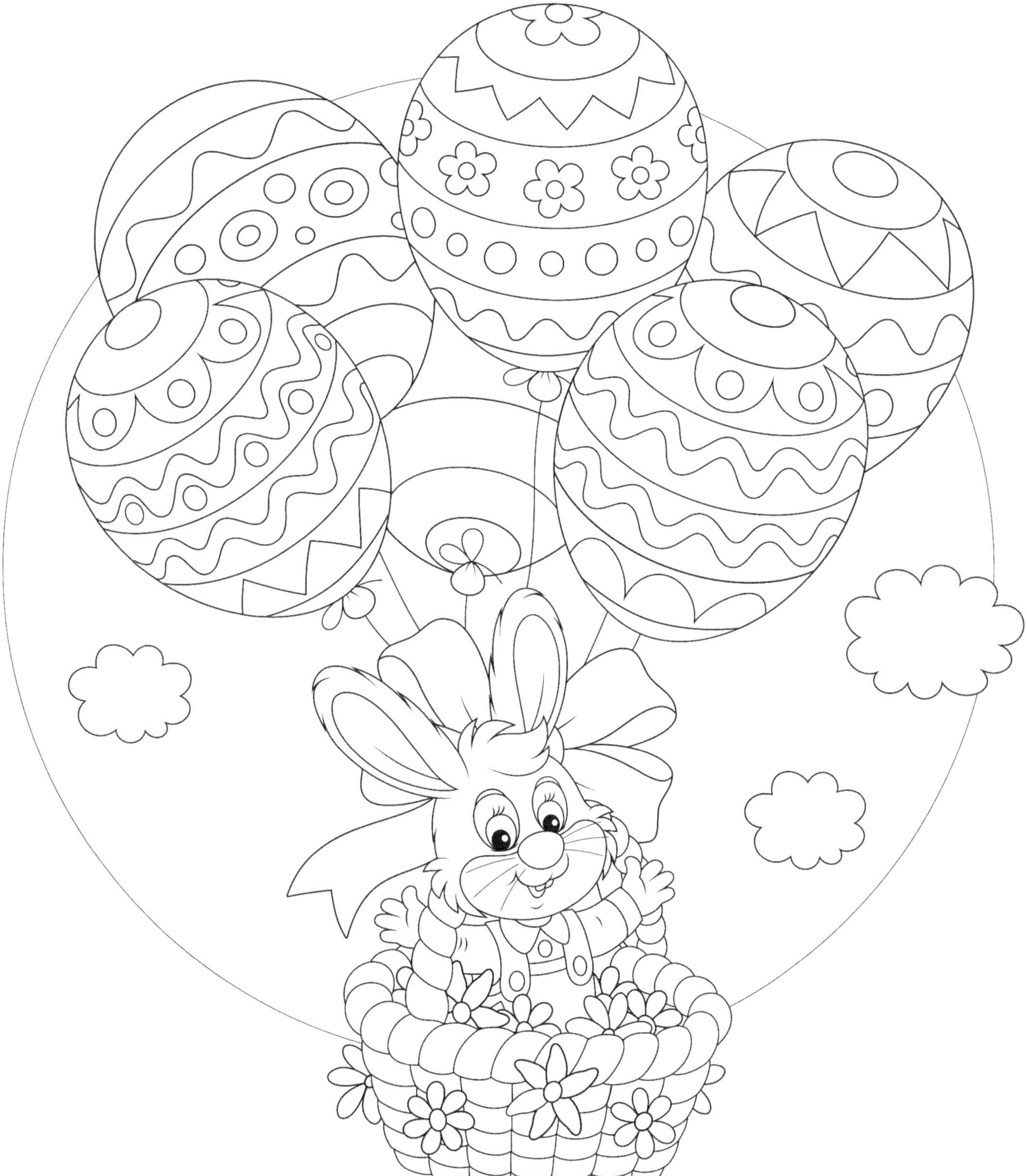

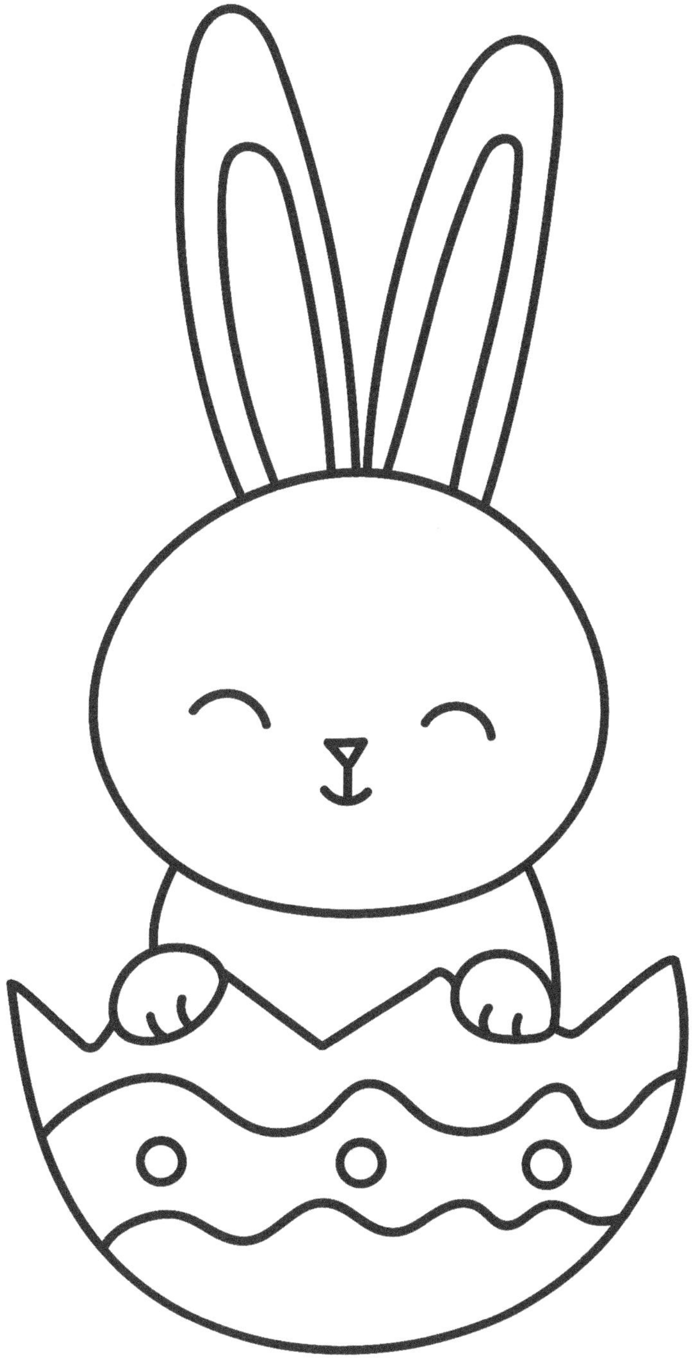

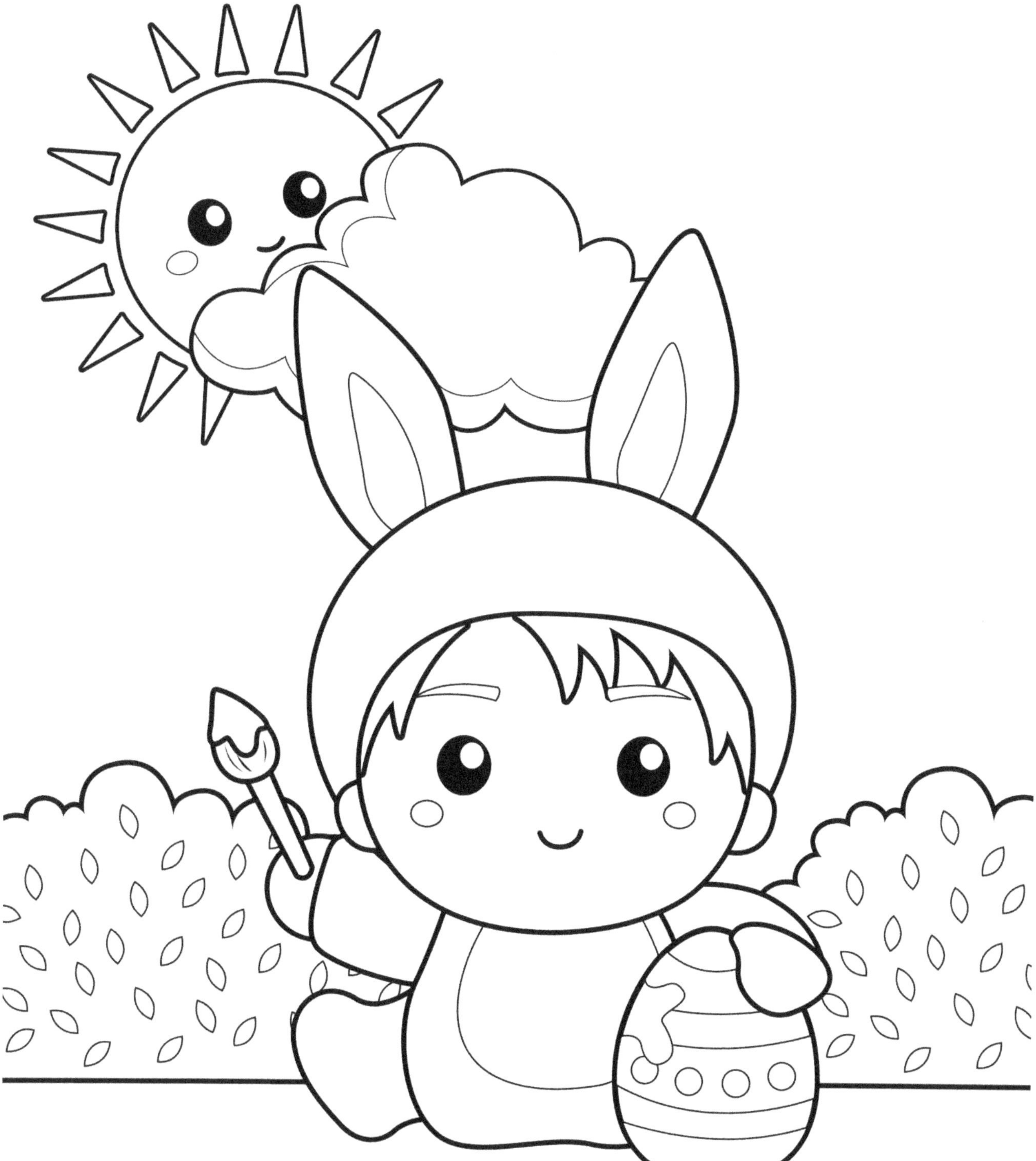

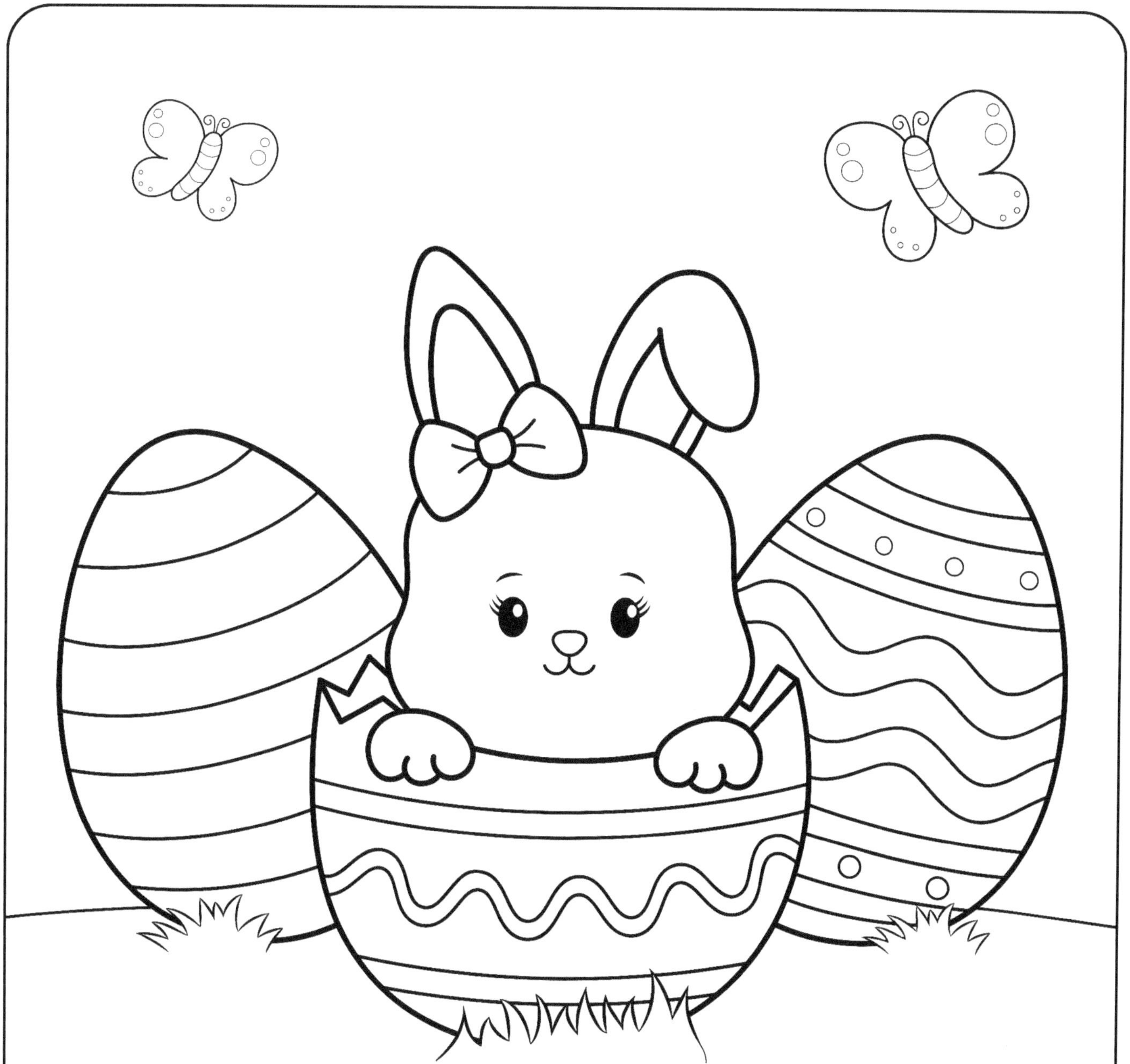

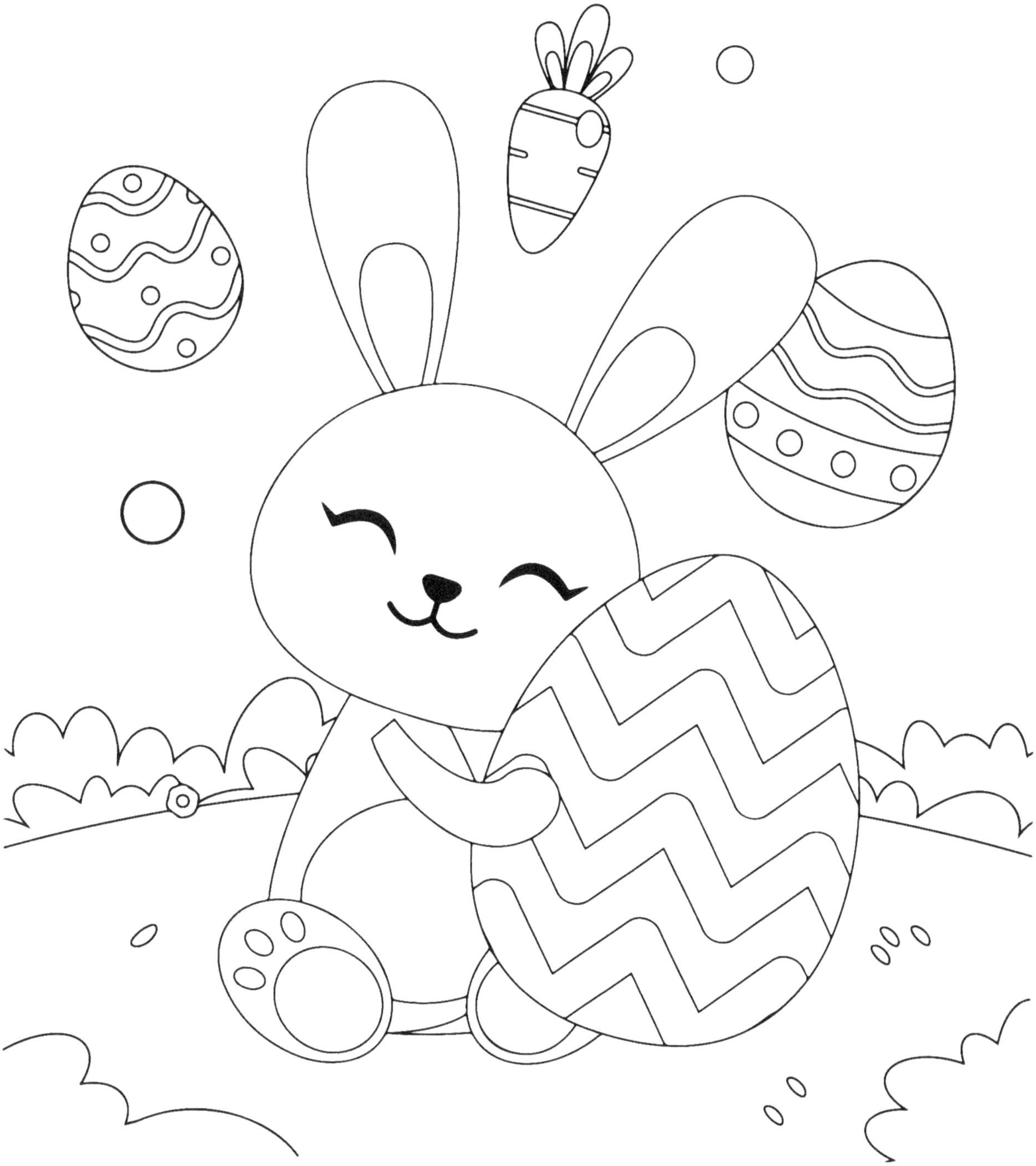

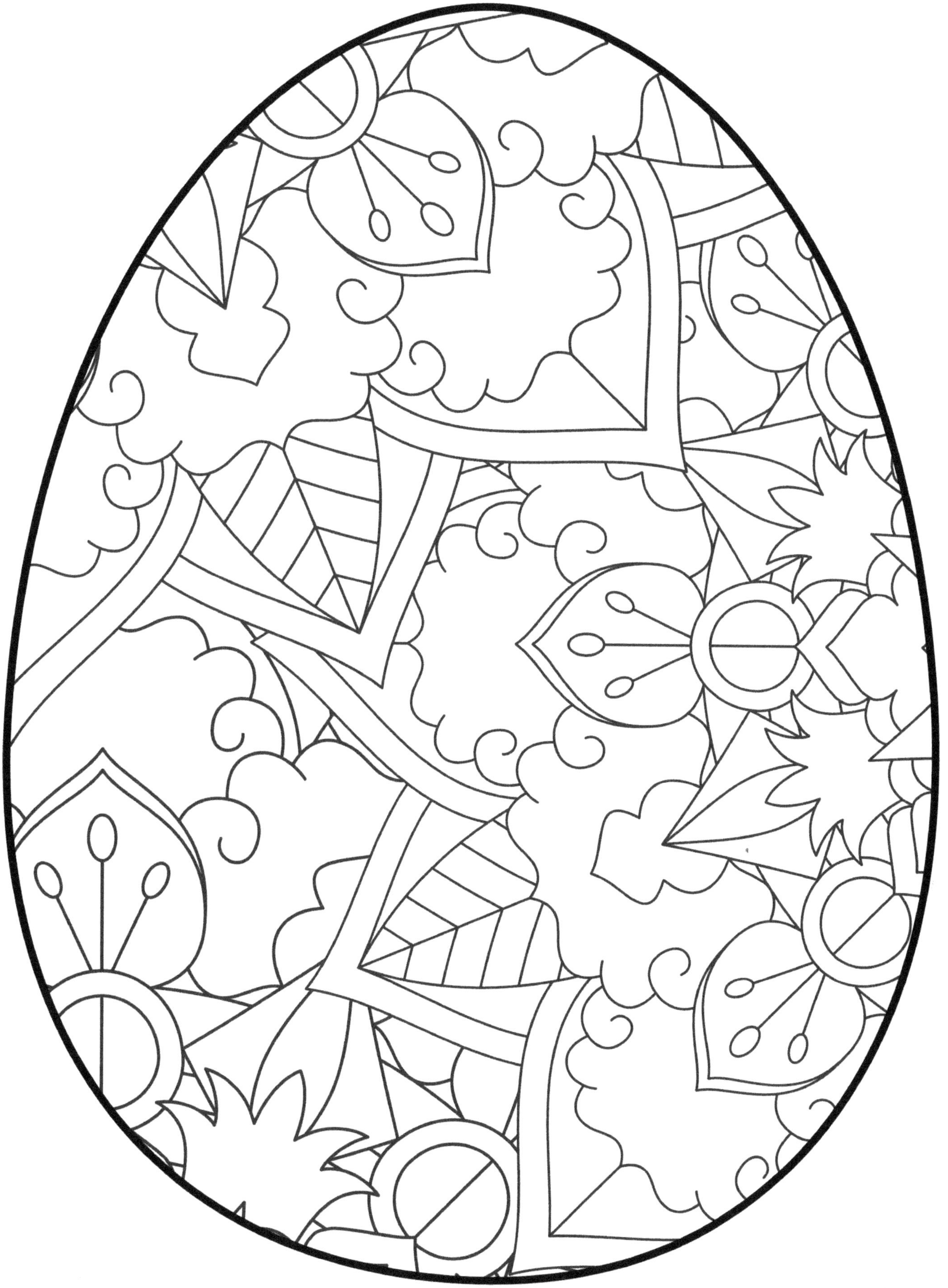

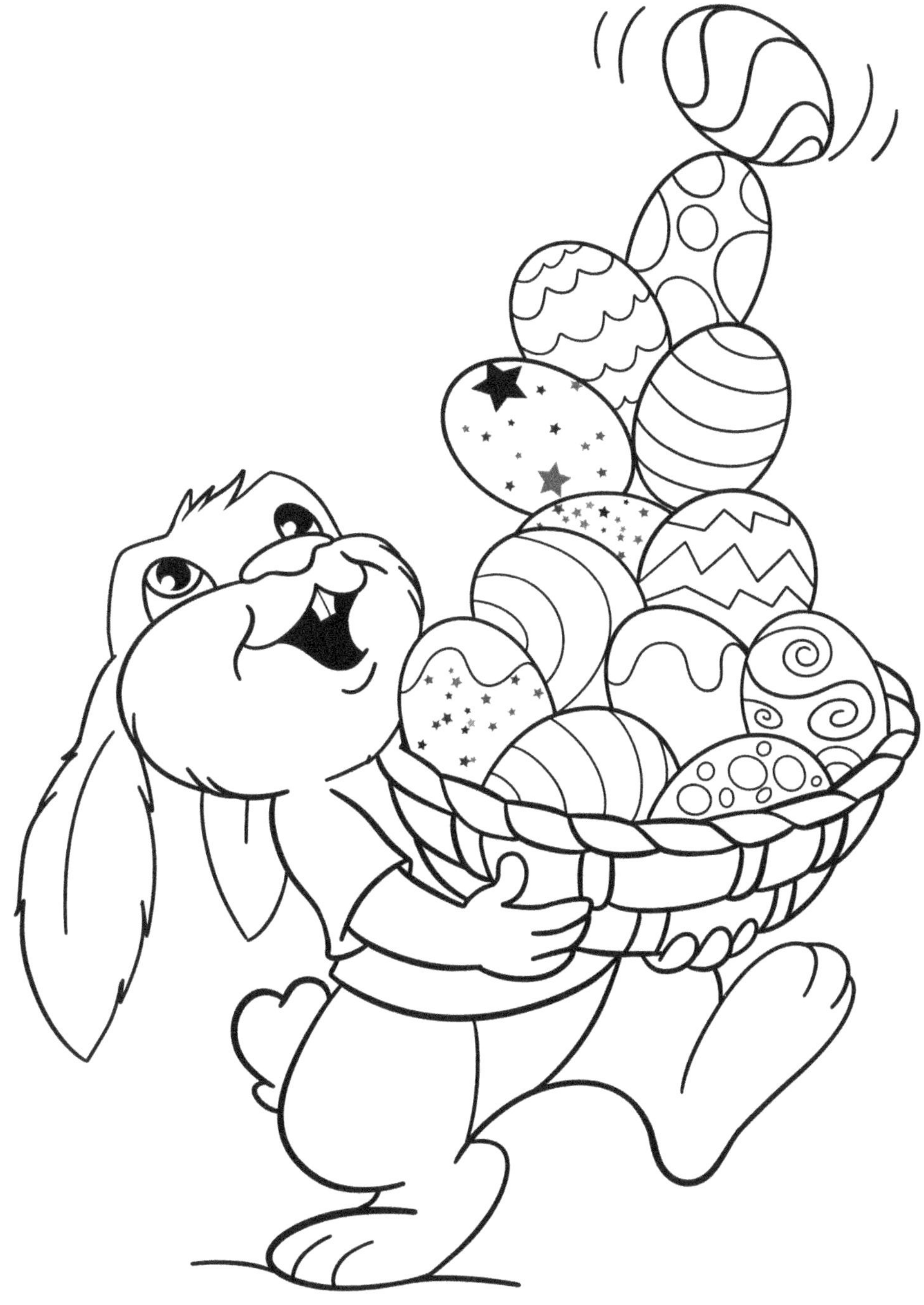

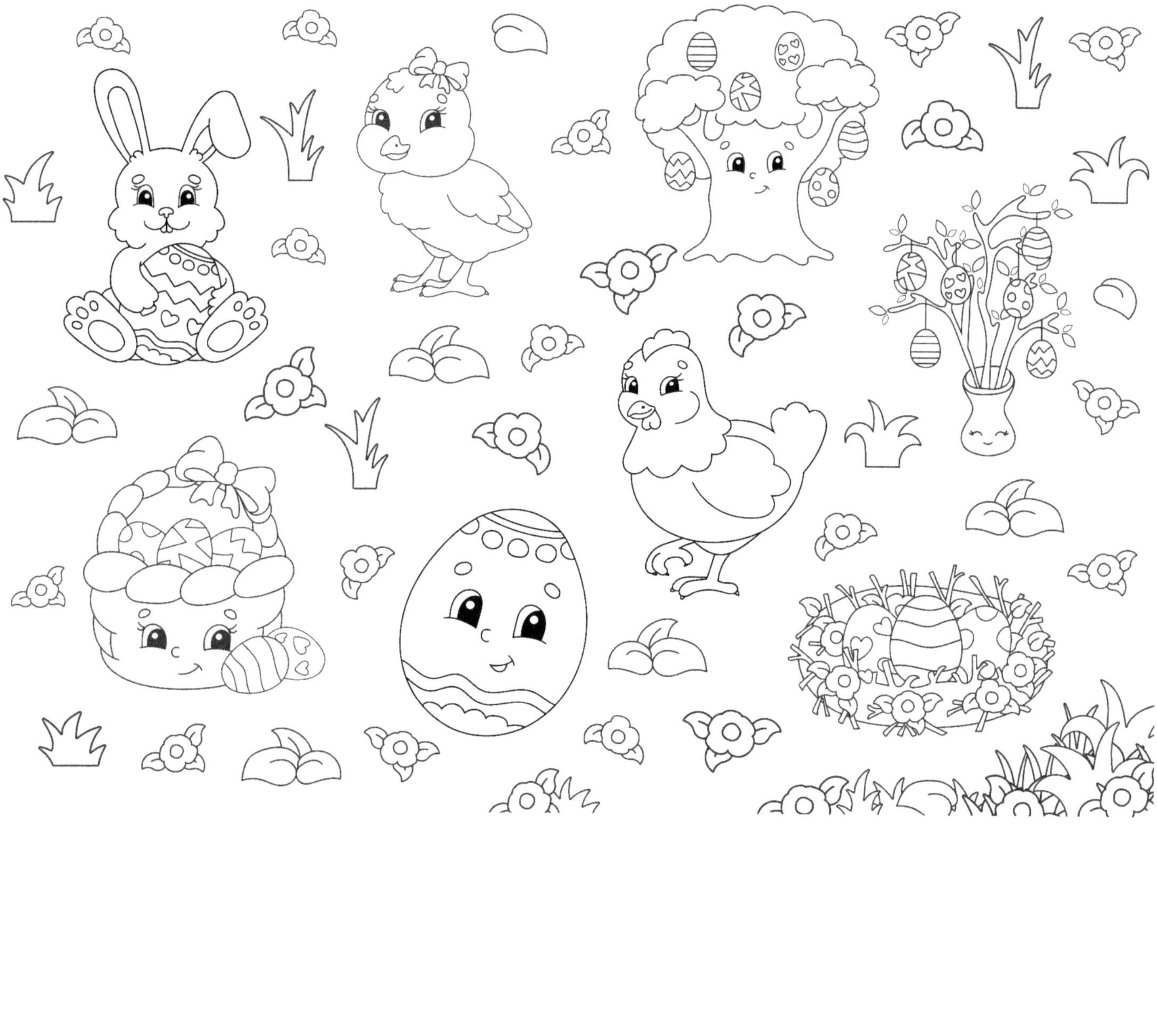

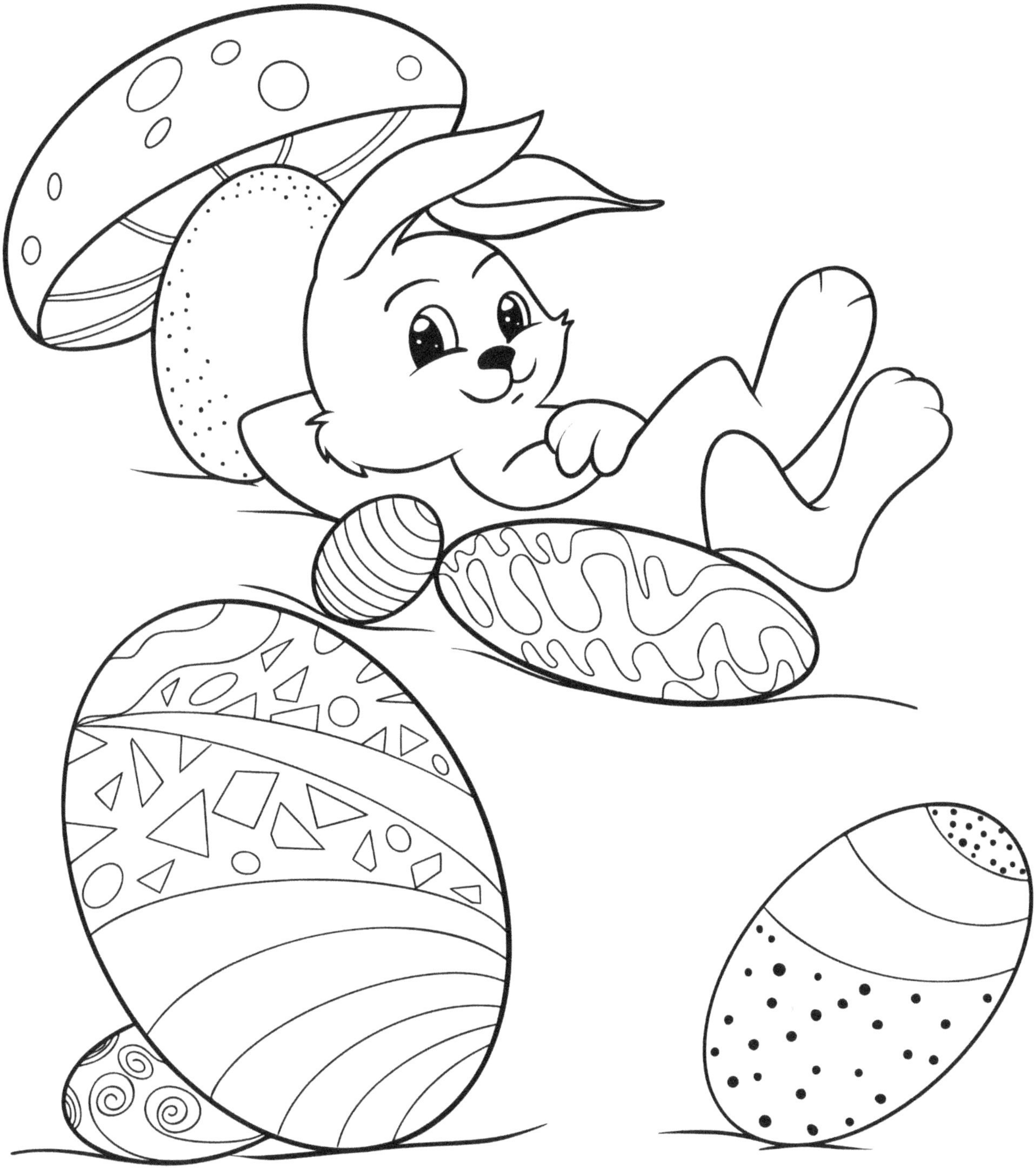

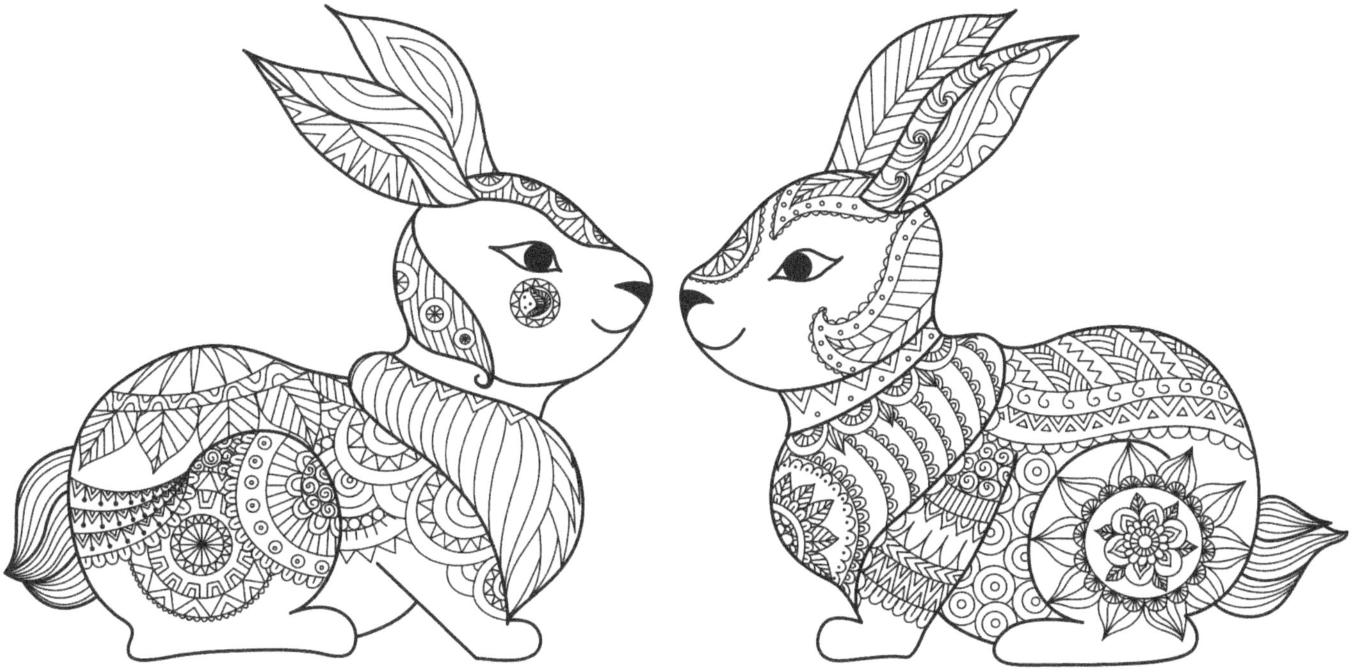

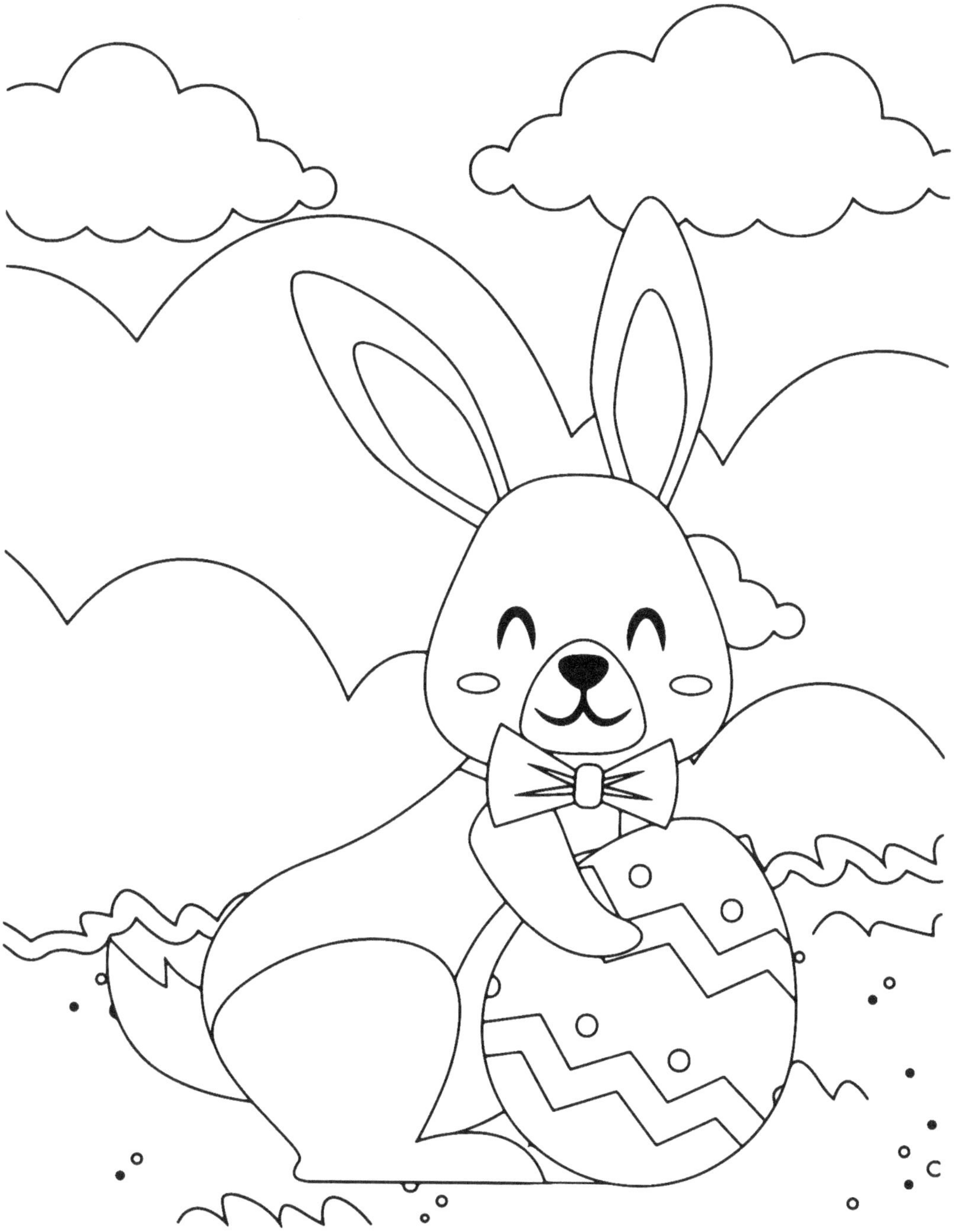

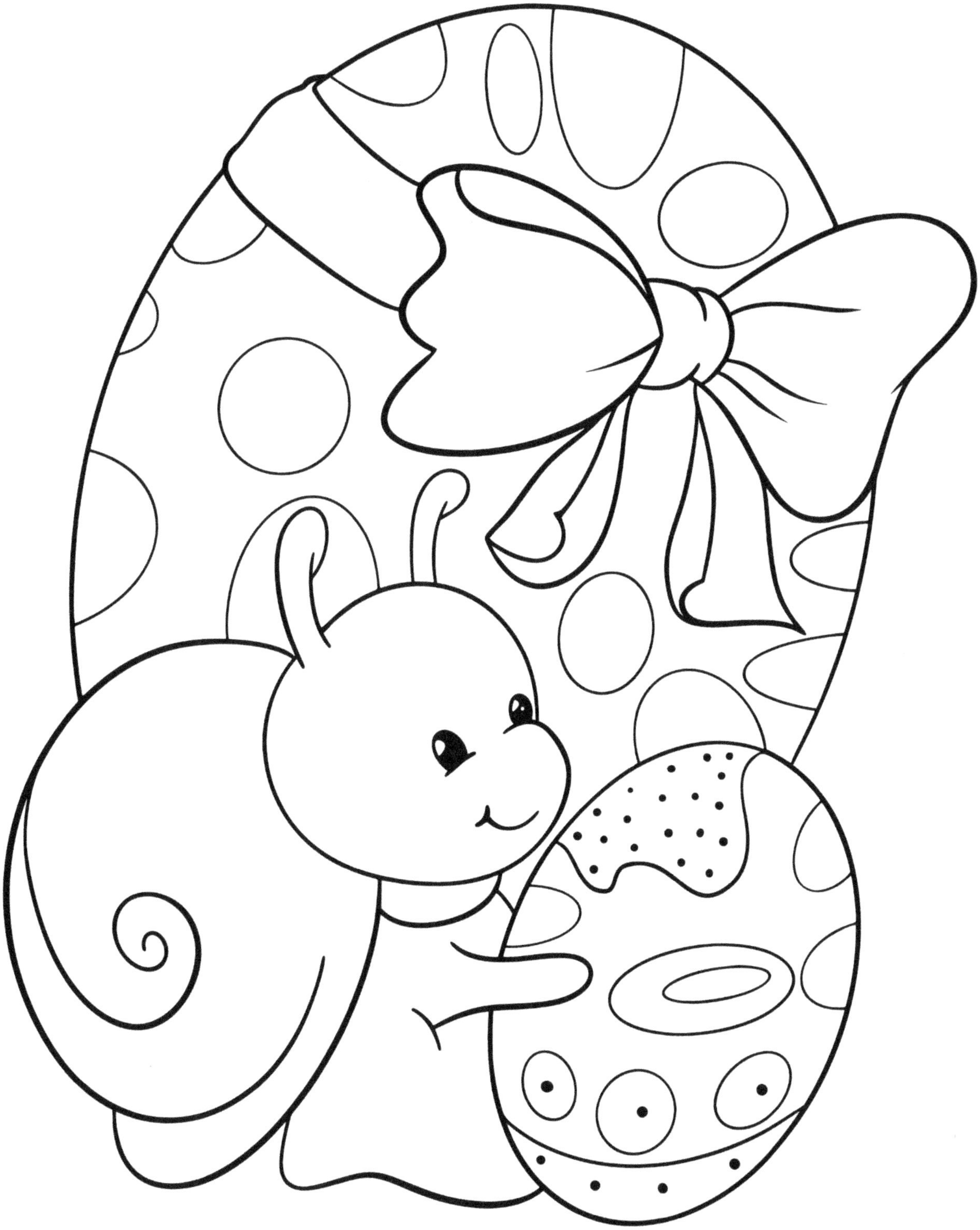

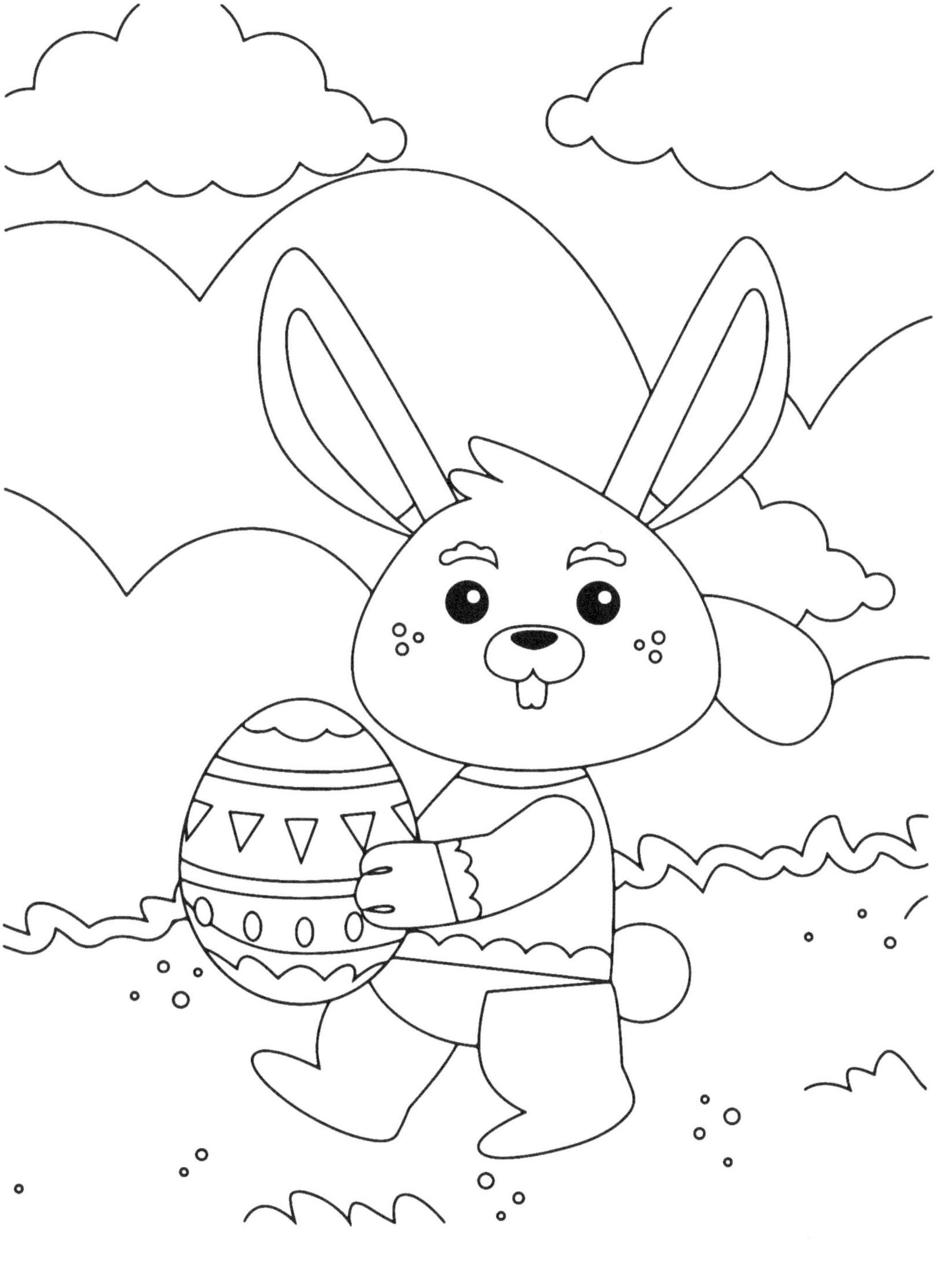

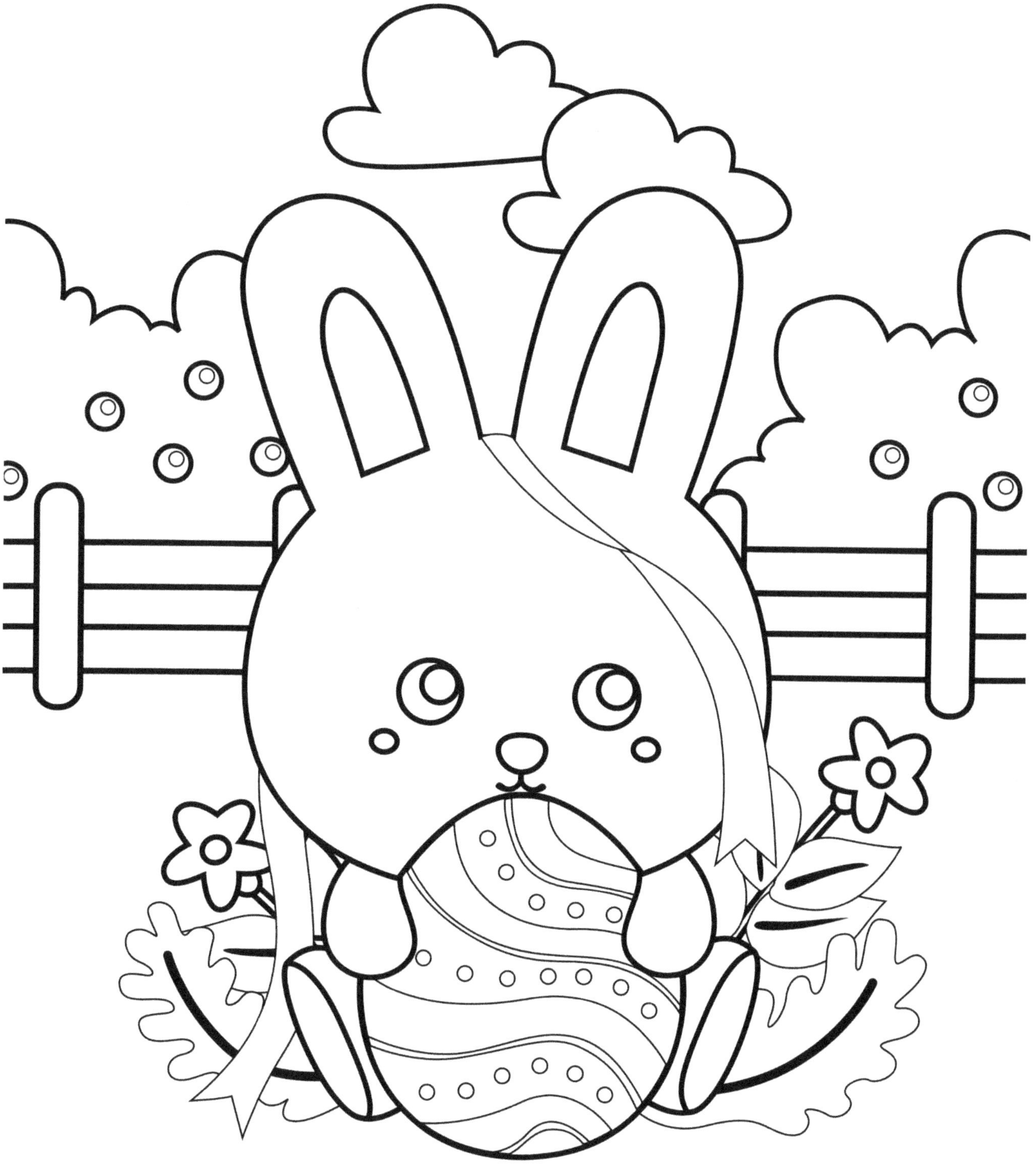

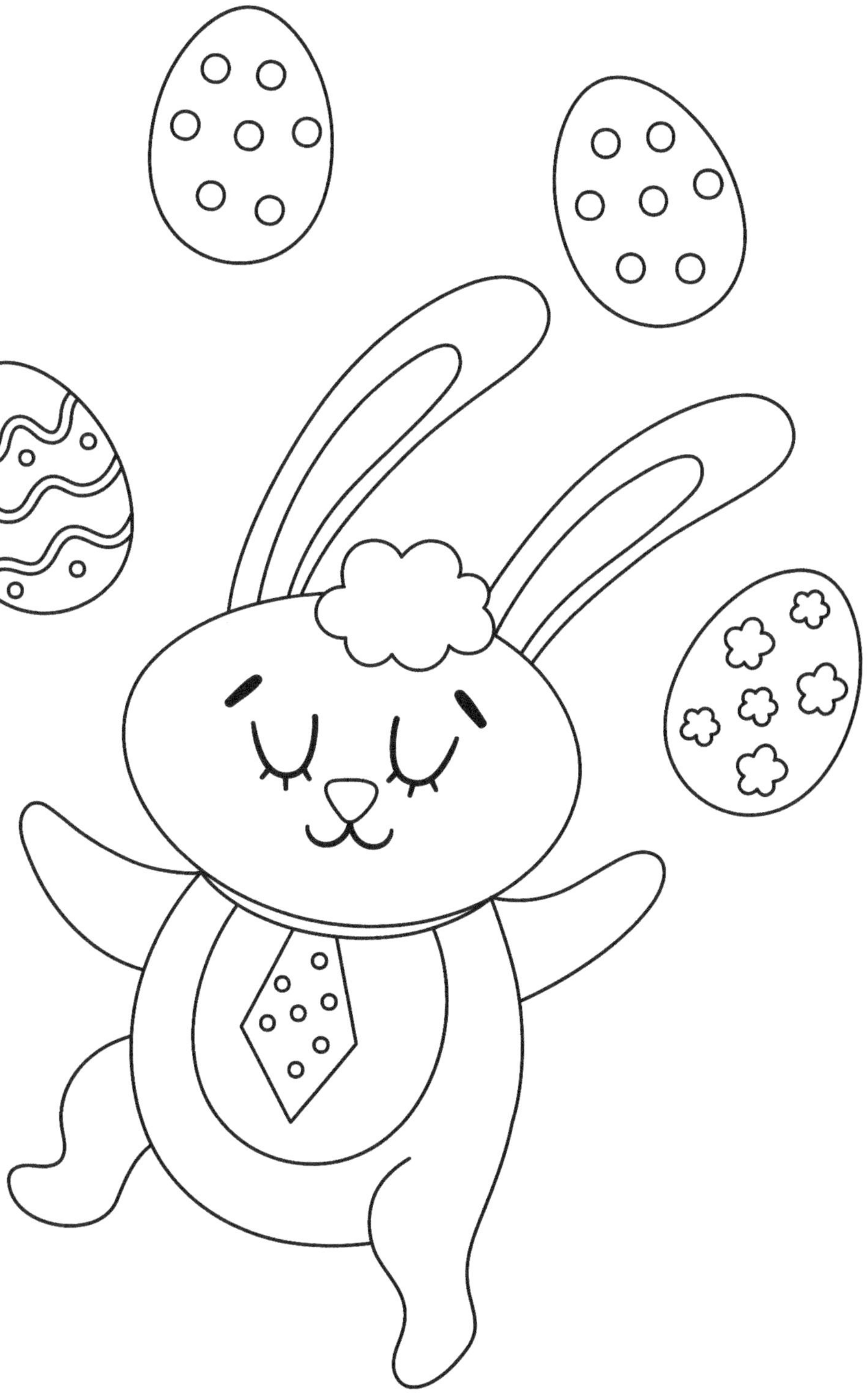

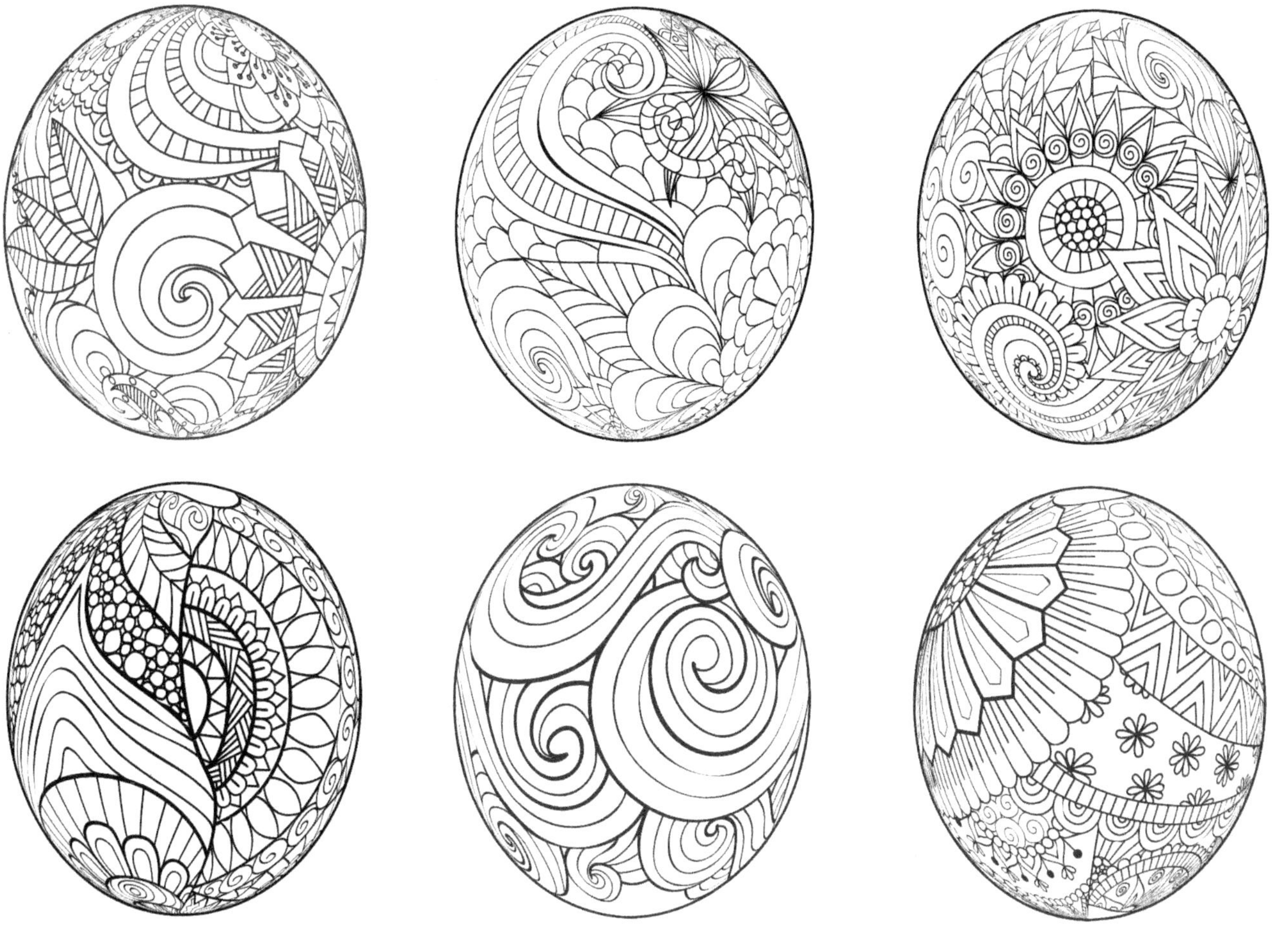

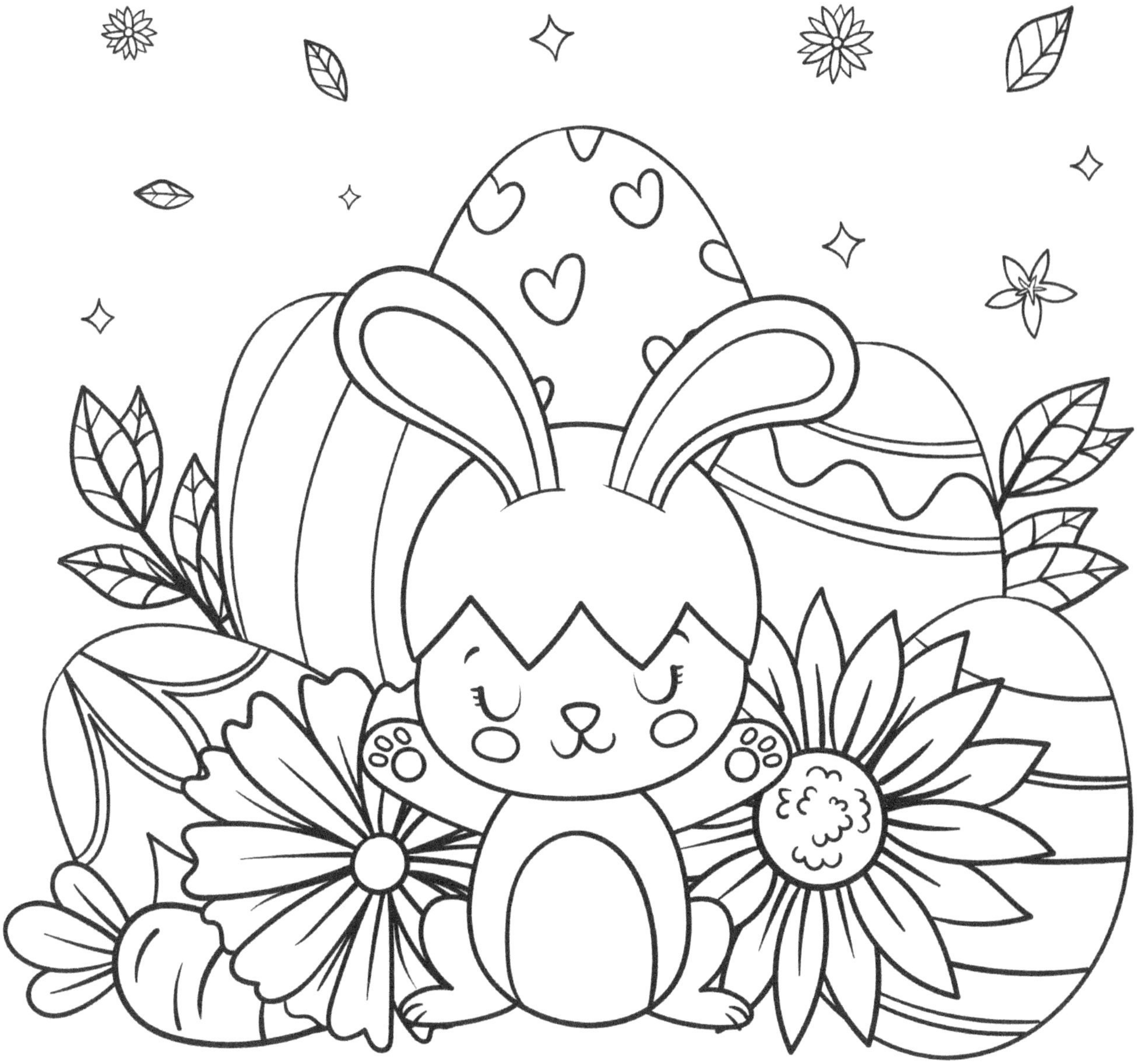

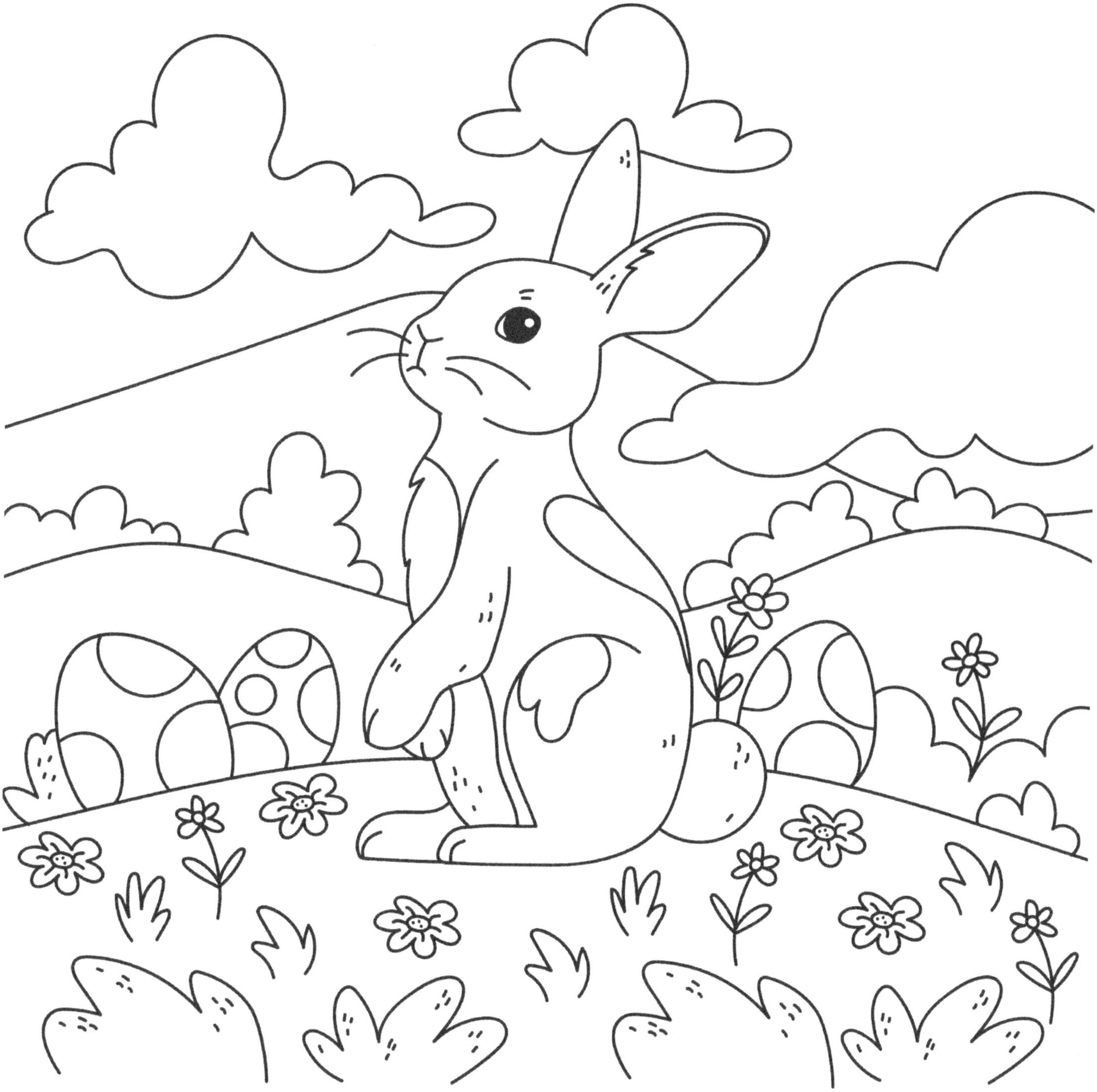

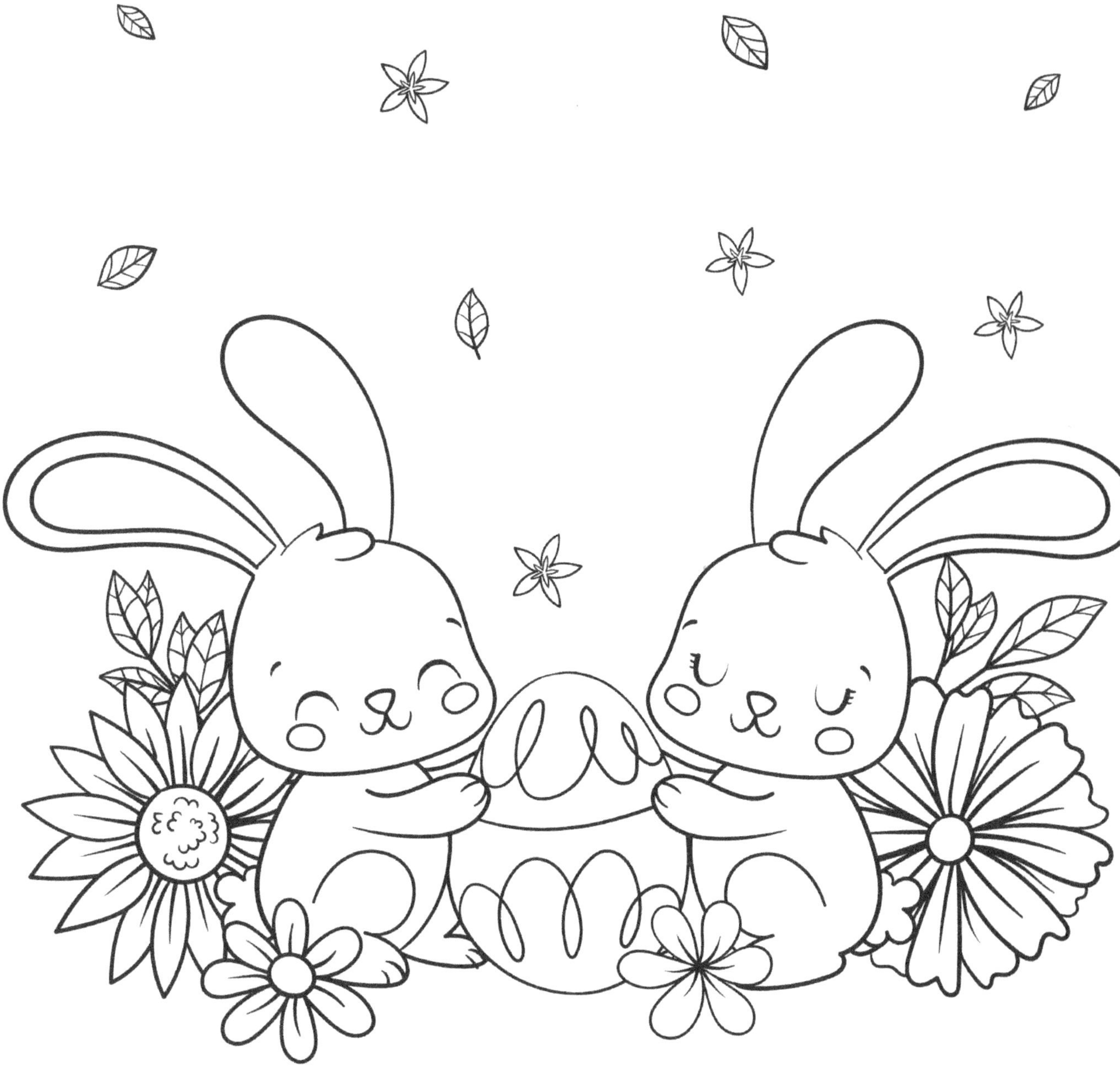

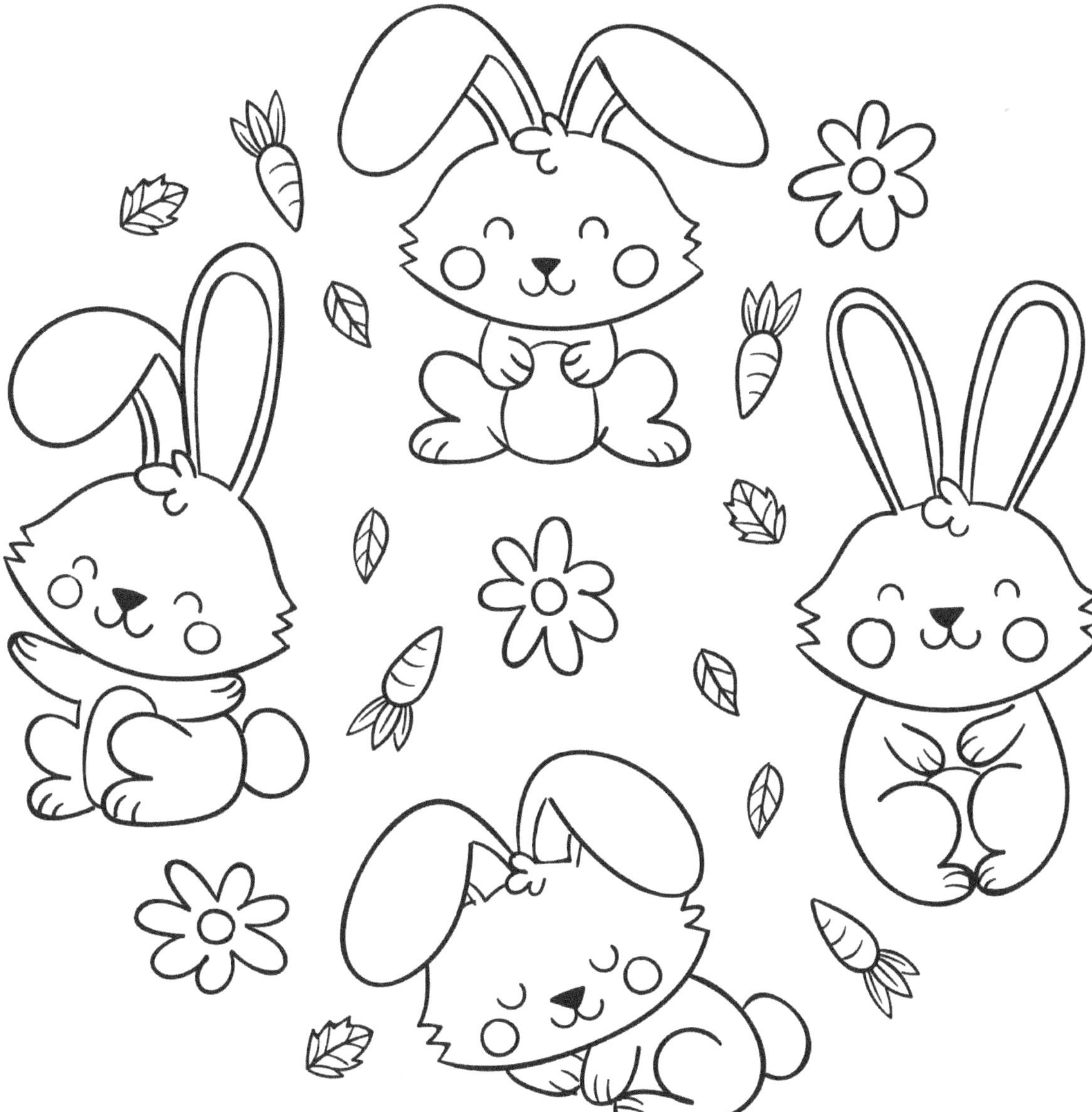

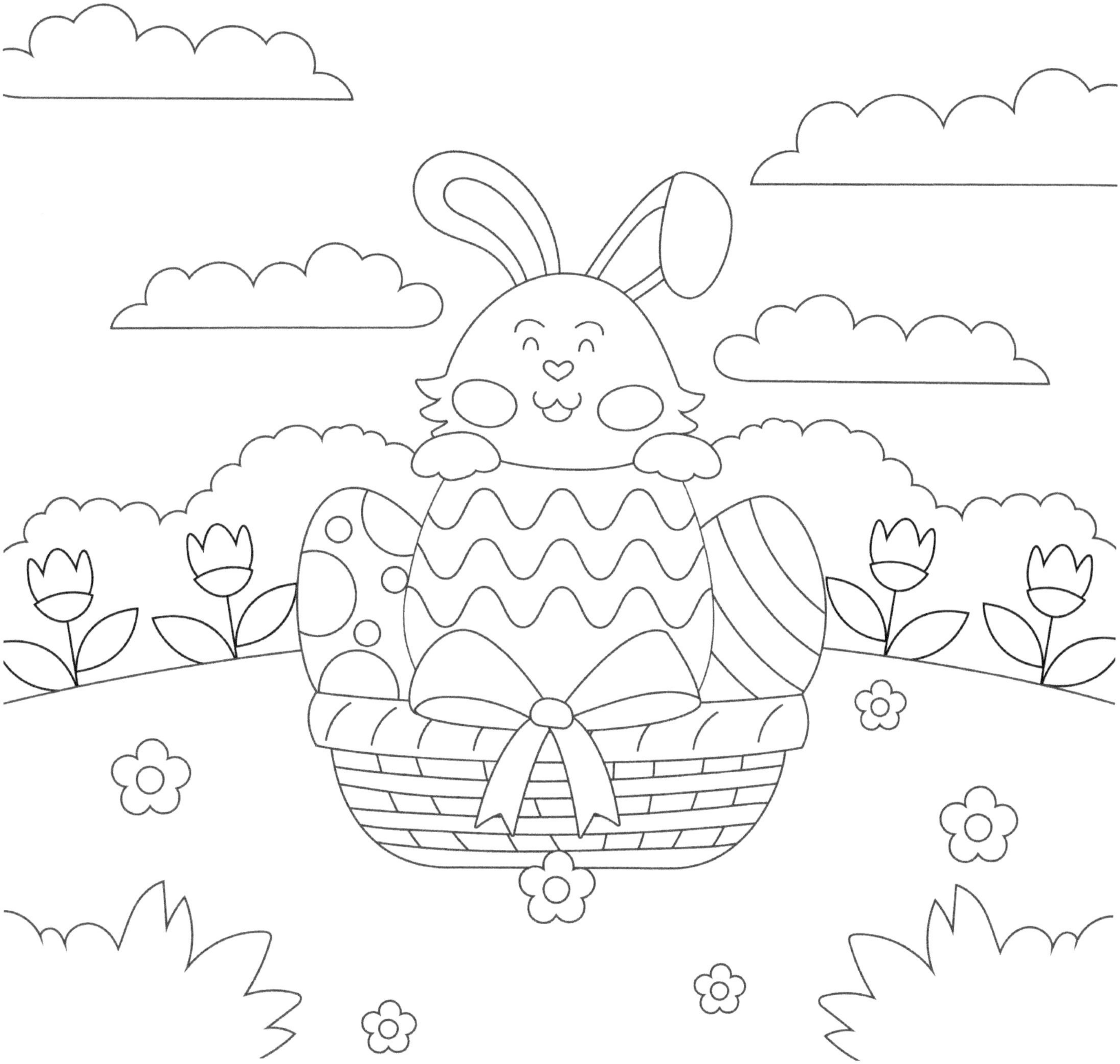

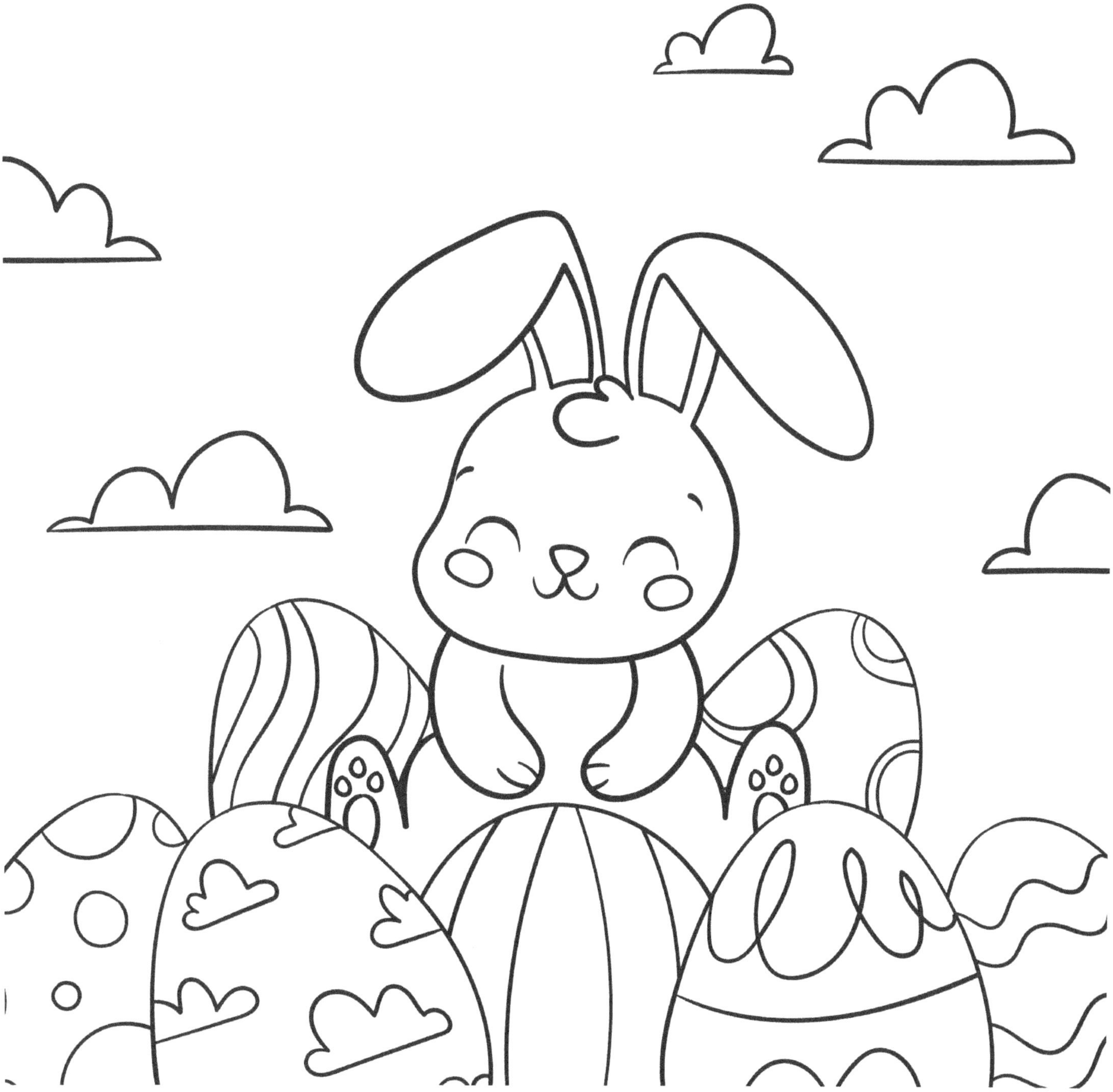

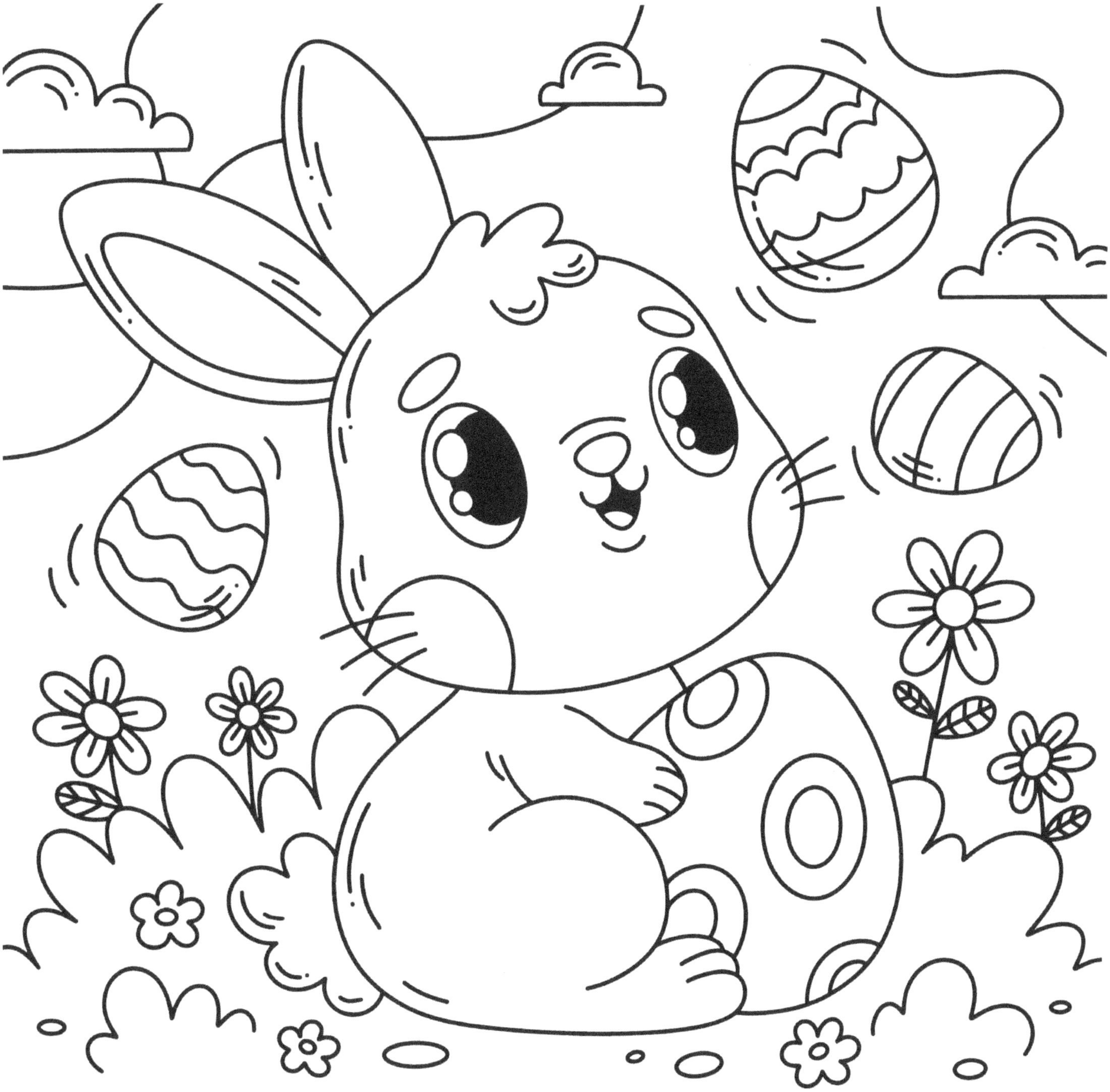

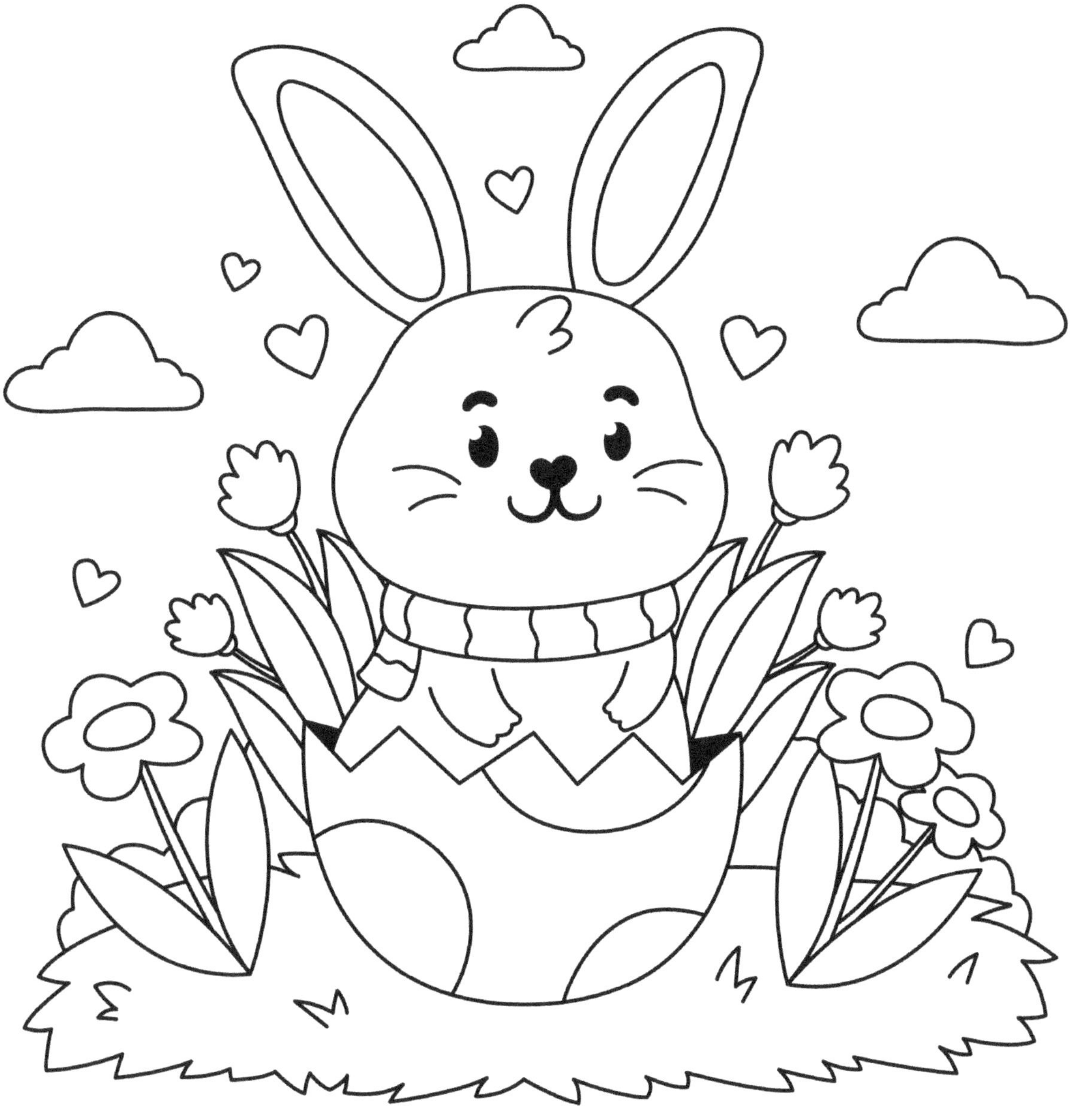

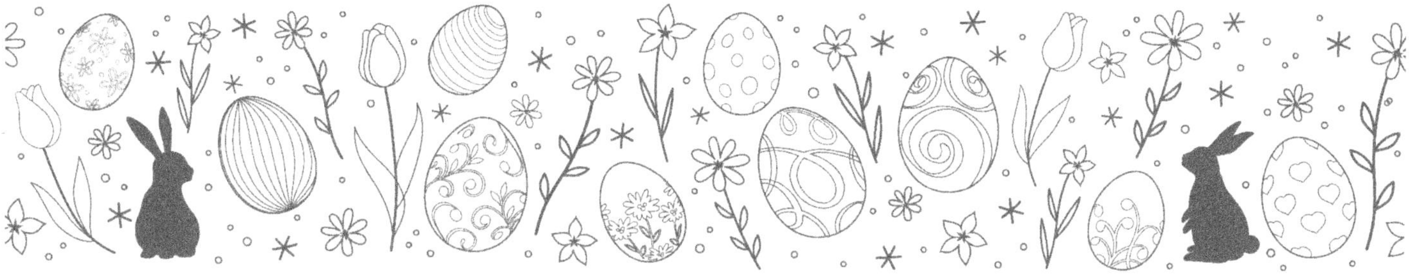

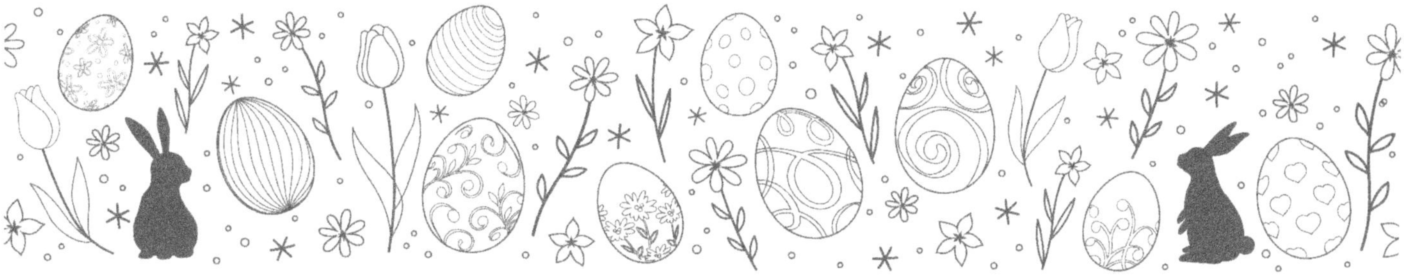

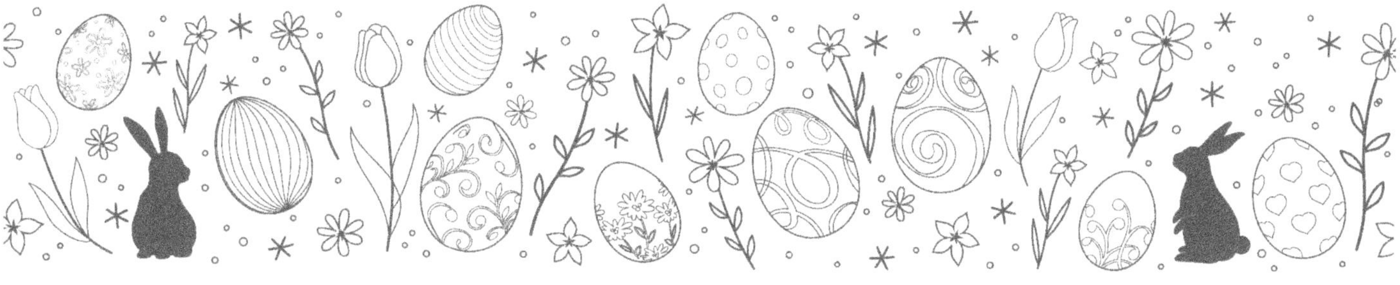

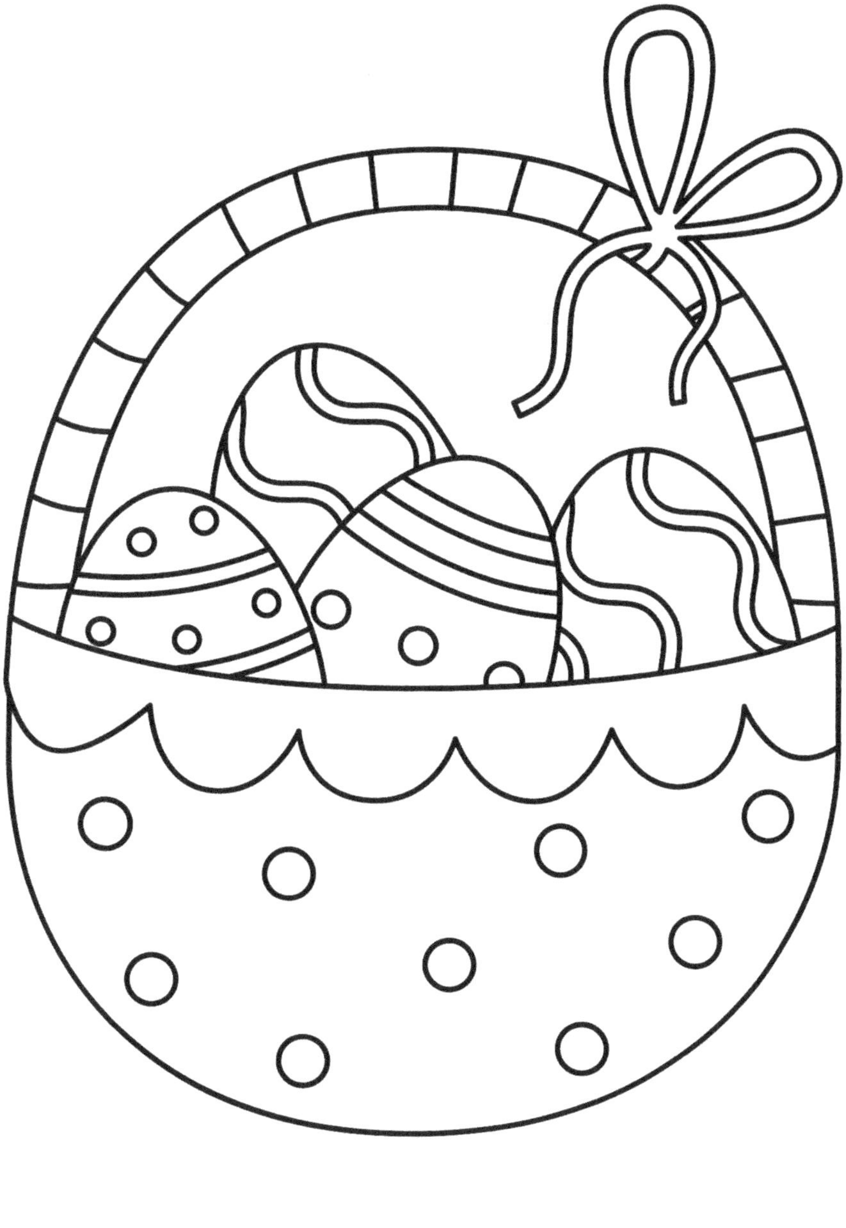

CPSIA information can be obtained
at www.ICGtesting.com
Printed in the USA
BVHW020841060423
661869BV00010B/221

9 798211 430709